NVM

YOLO

UNfollowED

IDK

?4u

L.L. ABBOTT

Books by L.L. Abbott

Lake Pines Mystery Series

Murder On The Water

Death At Deception Bay

Murder Of Crows

The Dead Of Winter

Anna Ledin Thriller Series

The Blackwater Operative

The Phoenix Code

Rogue

Blown

Teen & Young Adult

Unfollowed

Order From Karoo Bridge

Carole And The Secret Queen's Scarf

Genre Fiction

The Hotel Penn

UNfollowED

Just when you think you're
getting it right – it all changes.

L.L. ABBOTT

Cover designed by L.L. Abbott

L.L. Abbott
Visit my website at www.LLAbbott.com

Paperback ISBN- 978-1-989325-19-3
eBook ISBN- 978-1-989325-20-9

This story is dedicated to every teen – everywhere.

UNfollowED

Just when you think you get it right, it all changes.

JAYSON BARTHOLOMEW ROBERTS ROUTLEDGE, 15
a.k.a. Marshmallow

CHAPTER 1

Jayson Bartholomew Roberts Routledge, 15
Social Profile: 'JayBart' Followers: 13 New Likes: 0

It's been seven months, three days and sixteen hours since Riley came home from the hospital, and still, no one will talk about what happened to her. Not honestly anyway. Every time Jayson would ask his parents what happened, they'd just dance around their words. 'She just needed some time' or 'don't worry Jay' would be the most common response, followed by a pat on his back before they'd walk away, fearing more questions from him.

His family was not like any of the ones on the talk shows that are on in the middle of the day. You know, where the family gets together in a room and yells and screams and then cries after they have spent the day blaming each other for whatever crappy problem they're having. His aunt always had those dumb shows playing on the television when he would go and visit his nana just before she died.

Instead, Jayson's family kept smiling when they passed all the neighbors as they went in and out of their house on their way back and forth to the hospital. Acting like whatever was happening to them was normal and not a completely shitty problem that every family hopes they're never in the middle of.

Jayson thought that their neighbors found out the same information that he did – the same way he did.

Online.

He knew that not everyone's parents were stuck in the dark ages like his were, and they probably were busy working the social media stalker net as proficiently as their own kids were. Jayson didn't tell his parents this fact, because even though he didn't like everyone knowing their family's problems, he preferred his parents didn't learn how to use social media and then feel obligated to set up their own secret profiles to 'keep up on top of things'.

That's what his mother always said.

She was just trying to keep up on top of things. Whatever that meant. Anyways, with Jayson's luck his fifty-two-year-old insurance executive father who thought socks and sandals were an inventive fall shoe fashion statement, would have more followers and likes than he did.

It was bad enough his younger brother, Shane, had 1,097 followers and would rack up an average of 35 new likes on each post he put up.

The whole situation wouldn't have been so bad if his parents left him alone and didn't expect him to pick up the slack with his younger brother. It's not that Shane was a bad kid or anything.

He wasn't.

As far as little brothers go – he was fairly decent. He didn't go through Jayson's things and he kind of looked up to him. Even if it was because he felt sorry that Jayson didn't have as many friends as he did, Jayson still liked the feeling, no matter how long it was going to last.

It's just that it wasn't supposed to be up to Jayson to look after Shane. But because Riley's "issues" took up so much of his parents' time, the responsibility of getting Shane back and forth to school and helping him with his homework was thrown on him just over half a year ago. He was worried Shane was going to quickly become a pest.

Didn't his parents know how hard grade nine was going to be?!

Jayson was looking forward to having the summer before high school to himself and without any responsibilities. It was going to be the last summer he had to hang out with his best friend before he had to move to Edmonton.

Edmonton! Could James' parents have moved further away? It was bad enough he had to move at all, but why did he have to move to Edmonton?

It was the one city their favorite hockey team always lost against and now he was going to move into enemy territory.

At the end of grade eight when James' parents told him about the move, the two friends devised a plan to get their parents to agree to let James move into Jayson's house so they would be able to go to high school together. After all, they were always hanging out at one of their two homes anyway – what would be the difference?

Neither Jayson nor James were what you'd call overly popular. But, at least they had each other, they'd say. They'd been friends since preschool and the idea of starting high school without James as backup terrified Jayson, even though he wouldn't admit it.

It didn't take long for both of their parents to trash the idea of James staying behind and moving into Jayson's house. So as an alternative they planned to spend each day of the summer hanging out and doing all their favorite things before James had to leave at the end of August.

Top of their list was going to the private fort they had built in the mound of brush in the middle of the park two blocks from Jayson's house. Only they knew where it was. Together they dragged old bottle crates and two faded and cracked plastic lawn chairs, one with a broken leg. They perched the leg on three perfectly flat stacked rocks that took them all day of scouring the edge of the Assiniboine River to find.

They had covered their sanctuary with a dark blue tarp Jayson dragged out of their backyard shed. His father had used it when their roof leaked, but once his dad had it repaired, it had been forgotten and tossed in the back of the shed. Now at least it could be put to good use keeping their fort hidden from other kids and dry from any rain or snow.

It was in their fort, their sanctuary, that they could admit their fears, their secret crushes and even try a sip of a stolen beer from their parent's stash. Which they did only once but admitted to doing way more often.

There was no single defining moment that Jayson could remember when he and James became classified as unpopular. If he had to pick a year, Jayson would have to say that it was probably in grade six that everything began to change. Classmates went from celebrating birthday parties with every student in the class to just including a few friends, and teachers no longer insisted that everyone is included in holiday card exchanges. Leaving kids like Jayson and James to fend for themselves.

Teachers always talked about how the school was a safe space. Yeah right! Behind their colorful posters expressing acceptance and reminding students that 'everyone belonged' lay a group of teachers who didn't want to see what was happening outside their classroom because they knew they'd have to do something about it. And there was always a group of kids that knew that things that happen in the playground, stay in the playground.

And no amount of touchy-feely, inclusive posters and catchy phrases was going to change that.

At least not for Jayson.

That became evident when the first day back at school from grade six Christmas vacation, their overzealous gym teacher had a plan to start a volleyball intramural program.

Participation was *not* optional.

Colored team shirts were donated by the local pizzeria and players were selected at random. Or so Mr. Hoilstein claimed. I guess it was just a coincidence that all the jocks ended up on the same team and kids like Jayson, who found movement among athletes terrifying and awkward, ended up on another.

Mr. Hoilstein pronounced 'hole-steen', didn't seem to have any sympathy for kids like Jayson. And you'd figure a guy who had a name that was so easy to make fun of, would've had a little sympathy.

Nope. Nada. None.

Kids would devise names that combined 'hole' or 'steen' with other amusing words that commonly would make them laugh.

Never to his face; however.

This is how, Jayson was sure, he got on the wrong side of Mr. Hoilstein at the beginning of his grade six-year.

Now, it's important to know that Jayson tended to say things aloud that he was sure he was saying in his head. This is what his mom referred to as his 'switch', and she would claim that it was often turned off.

On September 18th it was apparently turned off in gym class.

Mid-class Jayson saw twenty-six faces turn and glare at him. Each one forcing down a burst of laughter and pressing their lips flat to avoid a smile. It wasn't until James jabbed him with his elbow that Jayson realized that what he was thinking of Mr. Hoilstein (when he told the class they had to each complete the two-mile run in less than twenty-five minutes to pass the physical fitness test for the sixth grade) was said aloud.

This, Jayson was positive, is what set the course for the torment he received in gym class as well as set him up for the nickname that would follow him for the rest of grade school and middle school. And he hoped, not the rest of high school.

Team shirts were folded in a pile on the miniature benches that were lined against the walls of the gymnasium. It was where parents would try and balance themselves while cheering on their children or where they'd wiggle along, uncomfortably, while sitting through an excruciatingly long assembly.

Jayson was sure that the school chose to not add full-sized seating intentionally.

"Teams have been chosen at random and the lists are taped on the back wall of the gym," Mr. Hoilstein announced. "Find out what team you're on and then grab a shirt and get changed. Be back out in ten minutes and we'll get started."

A mad rush of bodies pushed through the slower kids to the back wall where they squeezed around the list of teams that was typed on a single sheet of paper.

Names were typed alphabetically and with Routledge at the end of the list, only placed before Zane, he was one of the last ones to figure out what team he was on.

Random was not the term Jayson would use to describe Mr. Hoilstein's method of team selection. More like survival of the fittest.

Once he found out what team he was on he quickly found James' name at the top of the list and breathed a sigh of relief when he saw that they were on the same team. At least he had his best friend with him.

By the time Jayson turned and ran to the bench most of the shirts had been picked through. The remaining few were tossed to the side and laying on the gym floor.

There was one shirt left in the color designated for his team. Jayson pulled it from the pile and headed for the locker room.

Most of his class had already changed and were now grabbing a ball from the oversized wire bin Mr. Hoilstein wheeled to the center of the room and were bouncing them against the far wall.

With less than three minutes to spare, Jayson slipped into the locker room and began to get changed. He pulled the shirt over his shoulders and after he tugged it down over the top of his shorts, he ran out to find James.

It took less than five steps before he heard the jeers and giggles coming from the back of the gym. He wasn't sure who said it first, but once it was said, it spread like wildfire.

"He looks like a marshmallow!"

Jayson looked down at the tight-fitting stark white shirt that clung to his body and tugged at the hem but the synthetic material, reluctant to loosen, snapped back into place.

Jayson pleaded with Mr. Hoilstein for another top, "There has to be another shirt."

"It's not *too* bad," Mr. Hoilstein waved his hand in the air. "Just give it a tug or two and it'll loosen up."

That was all it took to push Jayson from the bottom of the social standing ladder deep into the sludge where only the kids with unflattering nicknames lived.

At the end of the day, Jayson ran from the school and dove into the back seat of his mom's car, choosing to not even wait for James as he packed up his bag.

James and Shane pushed through the school doors at the same time and ran towards the car. Shane sprang into the front seat, with a grinning smile and kissed their mom, and James took the seat beside Jayson in the back.

"I was looking for you," James punched Jayson's arm in jest. "You ditching me?"

Jayson shook his head, "No, just wanted to get out of there."

James nodded. He knew exactly why Jayson wanted to avoid the kids in the class. That was one of the benefits of having a best friend. You never needed to explain why you were feeling crappy because he always got it.

They rode the rest of the way home in silence. After they dropped James off at his house, Jayson pulled out his phone and began scanning his social media account, hoping that his new nickname wasn't making the rounds.

As he scrolled through the apps on his phone, he rambled off a flurry of Hail Mary's silently in his head hoping that Sister Mary Margaret was right and that if your prayer was said with candid conviction it would be answered.

Instead, he saw the post at the top of his feed. #marshmallow was trending in the group he followed. And there in the first post was a like from one of Jayson's thirteen followers. 'ShaneR', his little brother that sat innocently in the front seat babbling about his awesome day to their mom had liked one of the posts.

Jayson shoved his phone in his backpack. He knew that grade six was going to suck. He could just feel it.

He eventually learned that grade seven and grade eight would suck as well.

And as he pushed around the last of his cereal in his bowl, he was sure that grade nine was going to suck too.

CHAPTER 2

Grade nine was going to be the year that Jayson and James pulled away from the small group of kids they were forced together with since kindergarten. The same thirty kids that Sister Mary Margaret awkwardly explained the facts of life to in grade five and that Mr. McGuire managed to teach the new math to just in time to graduate.

"Hurry up," Jayson yelled back at Shane. "I'm going to be late."

"Okay, Okay," Shane shoved his lunch in his bag and then flew out of the front door and jumped off the top step of their porch and ran to where Jayson was steadying his bike.

Shane flipped his leg over the seat and began to peddle before both hands had gripped the handlebars.

"Helmet," Jayson reminded him.

Shane rolled his eyes and then squeezed the brakes. He grabbed the black matte helmet that hung from his handlebars and pushed it down on his head and then snapped the straps under his chin.

"There," Shane said. "Happy?"

"Whatever," Jayson mumbled. He began to cycle down the driveway before he turned right and then rode along the road next to the curb.

At the same time, Shane bolted across the front lawn, jumped the curb and raced down the street, narrowly missing Jayson.

Shane's school was five blocks from their home and only two blocks before Jayson's high school. The proximity convinced his parents that Jayson would be the most logical person to make sure Shane got to school on time every morning. Jayson disagreed, but it was apparent that it wasn't up for discussion either.

When they reached Shane's school Jayson slowed down just enough to make sure his brother made it onto the front lawn and to where the bike racks were lined against the wall. A group of Shane's friends ran over to greet him. Patting him on the back and high fiving each other as they slid their bikes into the metal slots.

Who high fives anymore?

Jayson shook his head and then rushed down the sidewalk hoping to make it across the street before the first bell rang.

Mid July a thick envelop arrived at Jayson's house explaining the rules and expectations for the students at Silver Oaks Secondary. And chief among them was the expectation that no one was to arrive late.

"Tardiness is not to be tolerated." Was the sentence that was typed across the top of the page as rule number one.

Who uses the word tardiness anymore?

Jayson could see students rushing up the front steps and through the doors of Silver Oaks Secondary as he was approaching the crosswalk. He looked both ways along the road and when he was certain no cars were coming, he began to dash to the other side. Standing as he peddled.

That is until a bright red flag was shoved in his face catching him off guard and sending his bike sideways and Jayson headfirst into the evergreen next to the sidewalk.

"Dismount!" came a scream from the pint-sized crossing guard supervising the empty corner.

"What the heck was that for?" Jayson crawled out from inside the evergreen bush trying to push the sharp branches away from his face. "Are you nuts?"

The kid waved his flag back and forth, "You have to wait for me to stop traffic first."

Jayson grabbed his handlebars and pulled his bike off the ground. He sized the kid up as he glared at Jayson like he had just broken out of prison. Waving his flag in his right hand, a neon vest over his bright blue fleece and a clipboard tucked precisely under his left arm.

This kid may even be more unpopular than Jayson was. No, he *definitely* was more unpopular than Jayson was.

"What cars?" Jayson yelled, but he didn't wait for an answer. He could hear the warning bell sound at Silver Oaks Secondary across the road. "Crap!"

Jayson jumped back on his bike and against the blaring protests of the crossing guard, he rushed across the road and to the bike rack taking the last slot available.

He squeezed his bike in the middle of the rack, and after a bit of a struggle managed to wrap his chain and lock around the front tire.

Jayson had memorized the location of his homeroom class from his schedule and as he rushed through the front doors, he was glad that he did.

Students were making their way through the corridors to their designated homeroom class. Jayson was among the shortest kids in the hall, a telltale signal that it was his first year of high school.

Size was just one distinction between the boys in their senior year and those in their first year like Jayson. Two others were body odor and the accumulation of facial hair, which seemed to directly correlate to the pecking order of the students. The beards, not the B.O.

Seniors took advantage of their size and seniority and walked shoulder to shoulder down the center of the hall, pushing the newer students towards the wall.

He wiggled through the mass of bodies and inched his way along the wall until he made it to the end of the hall.

Almost there.

He reached Room 123 and pulled open the door just as the second bell rang. He breathed a sigh of relief. He made it.

His relief, however, was short lived as he noticed the students in the class were twice the size as he was. He glanced at the blackboard at the front of the class and he saw 'Grade 12 AP Calculus' written in chalk.

"Crap," Jayson said aloud. The class broke out in laughter as their teacher turned around.

"May I help you?" she asked.

"I thought my homeroom class was in here," Jayson explained.

"It was. It's in room 145 now," the teacher pointed to the left. "You better get going."

Jayson ran, now through an empty hall until he reached the closed door of room 145. He opened the door and a room full of faces turned and stared at him. Some of the faces were familiar and none of them welcoming.

"Decided to join us?" Mr. Crane, his homeroom teacher asked.

Stout with dark hair and eyes, and looking closer to retirement than his father was, Mr. Crane was exactly how Jayson did not imagine his grade nine homeroom teacher to look.

The desks at the back of the room were all taken, and Jayson was forced to choose between the two remaining empty seats while the class looked on.

One was on the far side of the room next to Jonnie who Jayson had gone to school with since kindergarten. The second was next to a girl Jayson didn't recognize but was sitting in the middle of the room.

The girl had hair dyed a dark black, too dark to be her natural color with cropped bangs that covered the tops of her eyebrows, and she was cloaked in coordinating clothing. It reminded him of how Riley used to dress. He couldn't tell if the girl was wearing black lipstick and had her nails painted a dark black to match her outfit the way Riley did as well, because now that Jayson thought of it, she was the only one who didn't turn around when he walked into the room.

Jayson decided to take the safe bet and walked between the chairs and desks making his way over to the desk beside Jonnie when he saw it.

Jonnie's finger was pushing the side of his nostril around, stretching it as he searched for what he was looking for. And then just like in grade school, he flicked it under his desk.

It didn't take long for Jayson to change his mind and walk to the middle of the class and plop down in the empty seat next to Goth Girl.

Does anyone use the term goth anymore?

He sat quietly as Mr. Crane took attendance and raised his hand when he called out, "Jayson Routledge?"

"Here," Jayson called out.

"Do you prefer to be called Jayson or Jay?" Mr. Crane asked.

"Either one is fine," Jayson thought, then changed his mind. "Jayson is good."

"Or Marshmallow," a high-pitched voice snapped from the back of the room, followed by muffled laughter.

Jayson fumbled with the binder on the desk in front of him and noticed the school's name typed neatly across the front in thick black lettering.

Odd, Jayson thought, that the initials for the school were also commonly known as a signal for help.

He flipped open his binder and began to take down the notes from the board. Only six more hours and one hundred and ninety-six days to go.

Yep, grade nine was going to suck too.

CHAPTER 3

Jayson tossed his bag on the floor near his desk and then flopped back on his mattress. He grabbed a pillow from his bed and covered his face and screamed. He learned to try and keep his bad days to himself over the last seven months because his parents were so on edge. He couldn't tell them how much he was hating the idea of going into high school without his best friend or how alone he felt in a crowd of people his own age. He definitely didn't want to tell them about today.

The one time he did admit being a little more than freaked out about James moving away, his parents booked him in for a session with Dr. Sparrow to 'talk about his feelings'.

His parents were super sensitive to the benefits of therapy since Riley was found laying on the bathroom floor with an empty bottle of pills in her limp hand. The paramedics pumped Riley's stomach and Jayson could remember the sound of her retching as it echoed in the marble tiled bathroom down the hall.

His father told him to wait in his room and not come out. Shane was at a friend's house, so it was up to him, his dad told him, to listen and not argue with them.

There was something Jayson saw on his father's face that he had never seen before. Something that scared him. At first, he thought it was anger but as the months progressed in Riley's recovery, he realized what it was.

It was fear. Fear of losing a child and fear of not knowing what to do. He had never known his father to not know what to do, and here they were, faced with possibly the most important thing happening in their life and no one knew what to do.

Except for his mom. She was able to compose herself enough to call 911 and then direct everyone in their place. It wasn't until Riley was lifted into the back of the ambulance that his mom broke down and cried.

Over the last seven (and a bit) months the focus has been on Riley and keeping her safe and free from harm. Her regular sessions with Dr. Sparrow seemed to be helping and Jayson could see glimmers of his old sister returning to their lives.

His room was next to his sister's, with a bathroom between them, and across the hall from his parents. His brother Shane won the straw pull and took the room in the attic that both he and Riley wanted. In reality, the room should have gone to Riley, since she was the oldest. But she was never one to argue.

Since Riley came home from the hospital, she often took a nap in the middle of the afternoon. They had all learned to stay quiet between the hours of three and four. Jayson didn't mind but he couldn't help but think if they didn't want to talk about what happened to Riley, why did they have to change everything they did around her?

Riley was taking a year off university and focusing on recovering. His parents still wouldn't say exactly what happened with his sister, preferring to let the tense situation sit in hopes it would just fade away. But that wasn't happening. Even Jayson could see that.

A buzzing sound came from deep inside Jayson's bag. He tossed the pillow across the room and dove to the ground. It could only be one person.

He pulled his phone out of the bag and pressed his thumbprint to unlock it.

A text message was coming through.

JAMES:
hey, buddy – how was school?

JAYSON:
crap – u?

JAMES:
not bad....

Jayson couldn't help but feel a pang of jealously. How could James not have had a crappy day as well?

JAYSON:
u get lots of homework?

JAMES:
yeah, math is hard this year
u?

JAYSON:
Same

JAMES:
my english teacher already assigned an essay

JAYSON:
what u reading?

JAMES:
some macbeth play

JAYSON:
Cool

JAMES:
u been to the fort?

JAYSON:
no
shane wants me to take him

JAMES:
no!!!!

JAYSON:
ha! I know
r u still coming back at xmas?

JAMES:
yeah – u bet

JAYSON:
Good

JAMES:
k gtg

JAYSON:
kk
ttyl

Jayson put his phone on his bed and looked around his room. He had a couple of hours before dinner and had nothing to do. Normally he'd be riding around the neighborhood with James or heading to their fort.

He grabbed his bag and pulled out his math homework and decided to finish the assignment that was due for class the next day.

An hour had passed, and Jayson had finished all his homework. The aroma of rich lasagna wafted up the stairs from the kitchen accompanied by the scent of freshly baked garlic bread. Jayson learned to not get excited about dinners even if they smelled as great as they did tonight. His stomach, on the other hand, had not learned that lesson and began to growl.

His mother had quit work the day after Riley collapsed on the floor and was rushed to the hospital. Along with taking care of Riley, Jayson's mother also decided to take up experimental cooking.

For Jayson, that meant having shredded zucchini instead of pasta and a product that resembled bread, but that wasn't actually bread, instead of the garlic toast he craved.

Jayson grabbed his phone and scrolled through the feed for the day.

The first day of school came with loads of images of smiling friends reuniting after a summer apart. Some spending time at their cottages, others traveling with their family, but ultimately, everyone was regrouping on the first day of school to resume their social lives.

Jayson realized it was the first year since he started school that his parents didn't take a picture of him before he left. Not that he would have posted it, but it just seemed odd that it didn't occur to him until now.

He looked around his room and wondered what he could post. There had to be something.

He glanced over to his desk and sprang from his bed. He remembered the art class from grade eight when they had a guess photographer come to the class. He wasn't sure but he thought it was his teacher's brother who needed some extra paid work on his schedule.

Either way, Jayson remembered some tips from the class on how to take some artistic photos. He angled his phone along the rim of his desk and turning the camera a few degrees, he snapped an image of his homework.

A few adjustments to the filter and he posted it to his feed. He never added any text, mostly because he never had anything important to say. He just felt he should post something so he wouldn't seem like a complete loser.

He added three hashtags: #homework #highschool #firstday, then pressed 'post'.

When he was done, he scrolled through the images from the other people he followed. Most kids he followed never followed him back, but they were happy to have him along for the ride because it boosted their numbers. As much as it irked him, Jayson still found himself scrolling through their images, peering into the lives and friendships he was never welcomed to enter.

He went to James' profile. JamToe had fifteen followers, two more than Jayson. Jayson picked James' profile name and James chose his, JayBart. He looked at the images from James' drive from Winnipeg to Edmonton and was jealous of the easy-going family vacation that was recorded online. Stops at the large moose in Moose Jaw and the large Easter Egg (or whatever it was) in Vegreville were all used as backdrops for James and his sister as they transitioned their life from Winnipeg to Edmonton.

James posted a picture of the front of his high school. He too never added text, just hashtags. Jayson laughed as he read them. #homework #highschool #firstday. Same as his.

Jayson liked it.

His mother called up the stairs that dinner was ready. Jayson slipped his phone in his pocket and drew up the courage to face whatever was waiting for him on his plate downstairs.

As he was halfway down the stairs his phone buzzed from inside his pocket. He stopped midway and pulled out his phone.

One new like. It was from JamToe.

Jayson smiled, slipped the phone back into his pocket and headed to the kitchen.

CHAPTER 4

JayBart Followers: 12 New Likes: 1
JamToe Followers: 15 New Likes: 3

Day two wasn't starting out much better than day one did. After Jayson dropped Mr. Popular off at school, he raced towards SOS just as the first warning bell was ringing.

"Crap!" Jayson shouted as he peddled.

Mrs. Bolton shot him a stern glance as he whizzed by and he was sure she was going to call his mom and let her know what a delinquent he was.

Or maybe not. Most people were giving their family a break because of what they were going through with Riley. Except, Mrs. Bolton wasn't most people.

Jayson gave her a smile and a nod and kept cycling towards school. He was ready for the red flag as he zipped around the crossing guard, vaulted the curb and raced across the street. He glanced back and stuck his tongue out at the kid just as the sound of squealing tires echoed to his right.

"Look out kid!" came a shout from the driver of the miniature convertible as it stopped inches from Jayson's body.

Jayson stomped his left foot on the ground, but he didn't have enough of a solid footing to keep from falling. He managed to add an awkward hop and a high-pitched yell before he came crashing to the ground.

The bike slammed against his left leg and he winced at the pain that shot up from his knee.

His face flushed red with embarrassment as parents stopped to stare and kids walked around him as he struggled to get up.

He glanced back at the kid with the flag as he reached down and grabbed his handles and lifted his bike off the ground. The kid's fists were resting on his hips and the flag was pointing out behind him. His mouth was scrunched up and his eyes squinted in an 'I told you' sort of manner. He held his gaze on Jayson and then just before he turned around to resume his crossing guard duties, he quickly stuck the tip of his tongue out. Giving Jayson the oldest 'screw you' look he'd ever seen.

Yep, this kid was not going to be easy to like.

Jayson walked his bike the remainder of the distance to the bike rack. Again, he was one of the last ones to arrive and had to force his bike into the middle of the pile. The peddle jammed into his ankle sending a stabbing pain up his leg.

"Crap!" he shouted.

"Language!" The word came from behind Jayson. It was the voice of the newly minted principle.

Well, in fact, any principle would've been new to Jayson and anyone else in grade nine. But Mr. Felton was also new to Silver Oaks Secondary, or as Jayson was committed to calling it – SOS.

"Sorry, sir," Jayson mumbled as he worked the lock into place.

"Aren't you cutting it a little close?" Mr. Felton asked.

"Yes, sir," Jayson stammered. "I had to take my brother to school first."

Mr. Felton lifted his chin and looked down his nose through the bottom of his glasses at Jayson, trying to root out if he was lying or not.

"Very well," Mr. Felton concluded. "Run along. You don't want to get a detention slip."

"No, sir. I don't," Jayson answered as he ran ahead of Mr. Felton and directly to room 145.

His leg ached from his fall and from where the peddle jammed his ankle he could feel the small cut begin to bleed. He gritted his teeth as he hobbled into room 145.

"Making a habit of coming in late, Jayson?" Mr. Crane asked over the silence of the class.

Jayson shook his head.

"Take a seat," Mr. Crane pointed to the middle of the class where he sat the day before.

Once more, Goth Girl (Jayson never figured out her actual name and the moniker just seemed to fit) was the only student who didn't look up when he walked into the quiet classroom.

What was up with her anyway?

Jayson looked around the class for another seat and stopped when his eyes reached Jonnie, who was wiggling his nose. Most likely in preparation for a little house cleaning.

In the end, Jayson decided to stay where he was. At least Goth Girl left him alone.

The bell rang fifty minutes later. The scraping sounds of chairs against the polished linoleum floor reiterated the signal for the end of class. Chattering students gathered up their books and bags and rushed to their next class.

Jayson dropped his binder into his backpack, zipped it shut and flung it over his shoulder. Math was his next class and at least he would be on time for that.

He moved around the back of his desk and headed for the door when his bag slammed against something, or someone.

"Watch it, dork," it was Goth Girl.

Great. One more kid who didn't know Jayson, and that instantly disliked him.

"Sorry," Jayson mumbled and then headed for the door.

He was a few feet into the hall when a hand reached out and gripped his elbow.

"Wait up!" it was Jonnie and he grabbed Jayson with his picking hand.

Jayson shivered and was glad he had decided to wear a long-sleeved shirt today.

"What's up Jonnie?" Jayson asked.

"Not much," Jonnie moved up next to Jayson and walked beside him. "We're in the same math class together."

"Yeah, I noticed that," Jayson said as he tried to make it across the hall, pushing his way through the sea of seniors that blocked their path.

"Want to sit together?" Jonnie asked.

Jayson looked at him as they walked into the classroom, "Yeah, sure." At least Jonnie wasn't as scary as Goth Girl, and as far back as he could remember, he also never called him Marshmallow. If Jayson avoided sitting on Jonnie's right side, he would also be safe from any flying objects.

The morning math class went faster than Jayson had even hoped it would. Math was never a horrible subject for Jayson, but it was never his best either.

It seemed like high school teachers weren't as wound up as his grade school teachers were, and that the students were expected to hold more of their own responsibilities. This could be good and bad Jayson knew.

Geography class followed math, and so did Jonnie.

They were destined to be pals in school, whether he wanted it or not. Jayson could feel it. Jayson was able to avoid the lunch crowd on the first day by taking his lunch and sitting outside. However, he didn't think that he was going to be able to escape Jonnie or the lunch crowd in the cafeteria today. Halfway through geography class, the sky darkened, and clouds rumbled over the confines of SOS.

Rain began to pound the windows and it became evident that Jayson was not having lunch on the hill behind the school.

"What did you bring for lunch?" Jonnie asked.

Does anyone ask that anymore?

"Uh, some leftovers from last night. You?" Jayson asked.

"Peanut butter," Jonnie said.

"Didn't you read the rule book?" Jayson asked.

Jonnie screwed up his face, confused, "What'ya mean?"

"No peanut butter, no nut products. Ever," Jayson said. "It'll kill some kid who's allergic in our grade."

"Which kid?"

"I don't know," Jayson said. "Some kid."

"Great," Jonnie said, looking dejected, and then his eyes brightened up. "Can I share your lunch?"

Jayson thought about the fake lasagna and squishy garlic bread substitute and found himself lacking excitement about the prospect of his own lunch.

"Why don't we grab one of the burgers in the cafeteria," Jayson suggested.

Jonnie beamed, "Awesome idea."

They stood in line and waited for the five-dollar special to be served up on their trays. It wasn't the gourmet burger that his father used to sneak him out for on weekends, but at least it was a real burger.

Bodies pushed against each other as students grabbed their trays and rushed to find available seats in the cafeteria.

There is no place more important than inside the school cafeteria where you can establish and solidify your status and acceptance. Unfortunately, Jayson also knew, it is also the one place where you can establish your lack of popularity. Carefully coordinated seating could mean a seamless existence in school or four years of awkwardness.

Jayson was shooting for somewhere in the middle.

With their trays loaded with burgers, fries and a soda Jayson and Jonnie wiggled their way past the basketball team and stopped just short of the chess club table.

"Here," Jayson said as he lowered his tray to the table. At least they could eat their lunch unnoticed.

It took less than ten minutes for the fight to begin right behind where Jayson and Jonnie were sitting.

"Just don't make eye contact," Jayson said as Jonnie stretched his neck to see what was happening.

"But," Jonnie began.

"Eat," Jayson said.

Jonnie's face changed from curious to shocked as he jumped out of his seat and back three feet.

A fist came flying towards Jayson's face as he turned to see what Jonnie was reacting to.

Piles of bodies tumbled over the table where moments ago he and Jonnie were minding their own business while they ate their burgers and fries.

Somewhere in the mix, Jayson ended up in the middle of it and by the time Mr. Felton and Mr. Crane were pulling kids apart, there were a total of six kids in some state of brawl or participation with the fight.

Jayson landed on the floor, halfway under the table and a hand stretched out underneath offering to help him up.

He grabbed hold of it and was lifted from the floor and came almost eye to eye with the stout Mr. Crane.

"Jayson," Mr. Crane said. "Come with me."

CHAPTER 5

Detention was set to begin fifteen minutes after the end of the last class finished, which for Jayson was science. Mr. Felton and Mr. Crane were standing in the hall outside of room 367 which between the hours of 8:30 am and 3:30 pm was English Literature. At 3:45 pm it transformed into a detention hall. Jayson walked into the room and sat at a desk at the back of the room just as the kid who landed his punch on Jayson's face walked in.

Even if he hadn't been wearing the SOS branded melton team jacket, Jayson would have guessed he was one of the basketball team players. Jayson had to admit that the jacket was kinda nice. The dark maroon melton body was emblazoned with the SOS crest and the white leather sleeves donned the position, last name and number of each player.

He remembered looking at the picture in the school information booklet that came mid-July along with the marketing promise that you 'could stay warm on the sidelines and in between plays with this custom basketball jacket'. But what kids actually read was 'ensure an acceptable level of coolness with each purchase'.

The kid was about the same height as Jayson, but the comparisons could stop there. He had a dark tan, blue eyes, and light brown hair with gold streaks. He had a brush up cut that Jayson tried and could never manage, and the name on his sleeve read 'Moore'.

Moore had the type of swagger that came from never having been picked on or ridiculed. Crap! The kid even knew how to stand right. He joined his two matching teammates that were also hauled into detention along with Jayson, a girl he didn't recognize (but looked far from the fighting kind) and Goth Girl.

Great.

Who were the geniuses that figured they were the six masterminds responsible for the epic fight that broke out in the lunchroom on the second day of high school?

Mr. Felton then began to speak.

"I can honestly say I am disappointed in you kids," he was looking through the bottom of his glasses directly at Jayson. "It's only the second day of your first year in high school and here you are."

"Mr. Felton, sir, there's been a mistake," the suave comment came from one of Moore's teammates, although, Jayson was sure he wasn't referring to him or the two girls that were hauled into detention with them. The plea of innocence was reserved for the three jackets.

He held his arms out, pointing to his two friends, "We weren't even near the fight."

"Bull crap!" Again, Jayson's inside voice escaped. "That kid is the one who punched me! I was just eating my lunch."

Moore and his friends glared at Jayson, but the welt that had gone from red to a deep purple on his cheek since lunch hour was proof that at least part of what Jayson was saying was true.

"Jayson," Mr. Crane stood, crossing his arms in front of his chest. "Are you saying that Connor here is lying?"

Great, now the goon with the grin has a target on his head.

"I don't know who started the fight or what it was about, but I wasn't part of it," Jayson explained, hoping he sounded vague enough that he wasn't pointing the finger at anyone while trying to sell his own innocence.

Mr. Crane turned his head and looked at Mr. Felton and for a moment Jayson felt as if he may have escaped detention.

Then Goth Girl spoke.

"I was there, and it was that turnip head that started the fight," she stood and pointed right at Moore.

Turnip head? Who speaks like that?

Mr. Felton looked helplessly at the three matching teammates who were professing their innocence, "Do any of you have anything that would contradict what Sadie is saying?"

So, Goth Girl's name is Sadie.

The three boys looked at each other and shrugged their shoulders.

"It's a big misunderstanding Mr. Felton," Moore spoke, obviously adept at sweet talking his way out of trouble. "I think if we all apologize and promise to not do anything like that again, that we can agree that we learned a valuable lesson."

Jayson was all over promising not to get punched again.

Mr. Felton and Mr. Crane excused themselves and walked to a corner of the room so they could speak privately.

Jayson tapped his foot nervously on the floor, he was eager to get out of SOS detention and home as fast as he could.

Mr. Felton and Mr. Crane emerged with a smile on their faces. They had come to a brilliant conclusion that they were both proud of and eager to share.

"I think I have an idea that will work for all of us," he announced. "As you know from our information package, there is a zero-tolerance for fighting, tardiness as well as cheating at Silver Oaks. Not just because I abhor it, but because there was a huge problem over the last few years here at the school. When I took over as principal this year, I made a promise to the school board that we would stamp down hard on these issues with a tougher policy." Mr. Felton pounded his right fist on his left palm as he spoke. "So, if we can sit down with each of you and your parents, and make sure that we all understand that what happened is not acceptable and will not happen again then you'll be relieved of detention."

"But I didn't do anything," Jayson said, exasperated at the daftness of the situation. He then pointed at the quiet girl sitting two desks to his left, "And I'm pretty sure she had nothing to do with it either."

Mr. Felton shook his head, "Parent meeting, detention or dismissal. Those are your choices."

They were crap choices.

How could Jayson drag his mom and dad into school to talk about being involved in a fight on the second day of his first year in high school? They both seemed to be hanging on by a thread as it was because of what happened with Riley.

Jayson shook his head and mumbled, "Detention."

Mr. Felton's fuzzy eyebrows shot up in surprise, "What happened to your bravado?"

Jayson didn't answer, he just wanted to leave.

Mr. Felton then looked at Goth Girl who was standing against the wall, "Sadie?"

She folded her arms together and formed a thin black line with her body, "Detention, I guess." She bit her lower lip dragging her teeth across the dark black matte stain.

"Boys?" Mr. Felton asked Moore and his friends.

To everyone's surprise, all but Moore agreed to a parent meeting.

The last one left was the quiet girl sitting nervously in the corner. She was the only one who hadn't spoken, fought, or yelled.

"Lucy?"

"Detention, Mr. Felton."

Mr. Felton and Mr. Crane both looked at each other and shrugged their shoulders.

"Well, I guess we can call it a day for detention. Mr. Crane and I will arrange the two parent meetings and you four are expected to be back here tomorrow at 3:45 pm."

Everyone dispersed from the detention hall and scattered in different directions. He didn't look to see where anyone else was going as he headed straight for his bike.

The only benefit of being in detention today was having easy access to the middle of the bike rack. There were only a few bikes remaining and Jayson was able to unlock his without banging up his ankle again.

He arrived home before his dad and was able to sneak up to his room before his mom could survey the bruise on the side of his face.

He closed the door to his bedroom and pulled off his shirt and tossed it in the laundry basket. Somehow Jonnie grabbing him with his picking hand wasn't the worst thing that happened to him today.

He changed his shirt and then went into the bathroom he shared with his sister to see if he could cover up at least part of the bruise.

Riley heard him digging around in her medicine cabinet and stuck her head in through their adjoining door.

"What are you doing?" She whispered.

Jayson dropped the bottle of cover up he had in his hand and jumped back, "Crap! You scared me Ry!"

She walked into the bathroom and grabbed her bottle of make-up from the sink, "What are you doing with my cover up?"

"I thought you were sleeping?" Jayson said.

"I haven't napped since June," Riley confessed. "I stay up here because it makes mom feel better."

She wiggled the bottle in front of Jayson's face, "You still didn't tell me."

Jayson turned his face so the bruise that Moore gifted him at lunch was easy to see.

"Woah! Who sucker punched you?" Riley ran her finger over his bruise.

"Some clown in the lunchroom," Jayson said.

Riley's face lit up and she smiled, "You got into a fight?!"

"Sshh! I don't want mom or dad to know," Jayson took the bottle out of his sister's hand. "So, can you help me or not, Ry?"

Riley took the bottle back, "Turn around, you don't want to end up looking like a clown."

For the next twenty minutes, his sister cleaned, dabbed and primed Jayson's face and when she was finished, even he had a hard time pinpointing where Moore had slugged him.

As she worked on Jayson's skin, he watched her for the first time since she came home from the hospital. Any other time he felt like she would think he was staring at her or judging her. But here, he was able to really look at his sister for the first time since she tried to end it all.

And it occurred to Jayson that they were standing right where she tried to end it almost eight months earlier.

He wasn't sure what he would see when he looked at his sister, he just thought she would be different. In a way, she was changed. She would always be changed because of what happened, all of them would be.

But what surprised him was that he saw the same person he played hide and seek with when they were little, and hunted for Easter eggs with, and even fought with over the last piece of grandma's apple pie.

"Just keep that side of your face away from mom," his sister warned.

"Thanks, Ry."

"No problem."

Dinner was some sort of concoction of fake meat blended with salsa and wrapped in wheatless wraps topped with vegan cheese. Jayson thought it must have been his mom's attempt at tacos.

He didn't have the heart to tell her that she had missed.

He watched his dad choke back each bite and follow with a long swig of water, draining his glass three times through dinner.

“Roy, are you feeling alright?” his mom asked. “That’s your third glass!”

“Fine, dear. Fine. Just a little spicy,” his dad lied.

Shane escaped the evening meal because of his hockey tryouts and then pizza with the team.

Lucky little shit.

Jayson brushed his teeth twice to get rid of the ‘whatever’ taste that lingered in his mouth and then began to tackle his homework.

It was dark when he finished the last of his science homework and tonight, he just wanted to lay in bed and watch the last of the sci-fi movie he started to watch over the weekend.

After he changed into his pajamas, he hoped under his covers and turned on the television. His phone buzzed and made a hollow sound as it bounced on the top of his wooden night table.

He picked up the phone and read the message from James.

JAMES:
just got your message...
you got detention!!!

JAYSON:
not my fault

JAMES:
uh, huh...

JAYSON:
really
some goons fault

JAMES:
what happened?

For the next half hour, Jayson and James texted back and forth recounting their day to each other. Today would have been one of those days that he would have wanted to have James around. He tried to explain Moore and his goons as well as Goth Girl who managed to scare him more than Moore did. But it just didn't seem as funny through texts.

JAYSON:
wish you were here bro

JAMES:
u2

Before Jayson turned off his phone, he checked the feed on his phone.

JayBart Followers: 10 New Likes: 0

Jayson turned off the light and pulled the cover over his head. Only one hundred and ninety-five days left to go.

CHAPTER 6

Jayson woke up a half-hour earlier than he normally did and snuck down to the kitchen before his mom got up to have her coffee. His father was dressed, ready for work, and digging around in the back of the fridge. His father was over six feet tall and when his head and upper body deep in the second shelf of the fridge he looked more like a cartoon character.

"Hey dad," Jayson said as he walked into the kitchen.

His dad jolted his body up and banged his head on the interior light of the fridge.

"Damn it, Jay," he rubbed the top of his head as he crawled out of the fridge and straightened his body. "Don't sneak up on me like that."

"Sorry dad," Jayson said.

"What are you doing up so early?"

"Truth?" Jayson asked. "I am looking for something that I can put in my lunch that I can actually eat. I think mom packed some of that fake taco for me to have."

His dad let out a laugh and pointed his thumb at the fridge, "That's what I was doing."

And for the first time since Ry's trip to the hospital, he and his dad shared a laugh. A completely unencumbered laugh.

"I can give you some money if you want to buy lunch today at school?" his dad said as he reached into his pocket.

Jayson put up his hand and shook his head, "That's okay. The cafeteria food didn't sit well with me yesterday."

"Sorry to hear that," his dad took a swig of coffee. "At least she left this alone!" He said as he lifted his cup.

His dad grabbed his bag and keys and headed for the door, "Have a good day Jay."

"You too, dad."

Jayson skipped over the fake meat and peanut butter and made a sandwich out of cucumbers, peppers and hummus and wrapped it together with some organic juice and cookies his mom bought that wasn't half bad.

Shane was ready earlier than the two previous days and was eager to get to school. That was fine with Jayson because he didn't need another reason to have Mr. Felton eye him for extra detention.

Shane waved Jayson off as they neared the school and a group of ten kids was waiting for him to arrive.

Lucky kid. Jayson thought as he rode away and towards the gauntlet, he came to know as the crossing guard.

The kid, whoever he was, was also waiting for Jayson and had found his career challenge in corralling Jayson across the road.

Jayson pulled the straps on his backpack tight and leaned forward over his handlebars.

He switched his bike to a higher gear to make sure each peddle gave him maximum distance and powered towards his nemesis.

He saw the flag begin to wave when he was at least ten feet from the corner. The kid's frantic arms waved in the air as he saw Jayson barreling towards him on his bike, completely intent on not stopping at the curb.

"Dismount! Dismount!" came the cries from the neon flag bearer. The kid was relentless, Jayson had to give him that.

He was closer now, only a few feet away. Jayson could see through the intersection and to both the left and the right of the road.

No cars, and no buses.

Just Jayson and the flag.

The kid jumped in front of Jayson as he peddled towards the corner, leaving his post unmanned and unprotected. He was just as intent on keeping Jayson from crossing illegally as Jayson was on ignoring him.

Now Jayson was only a few feet away from the waving flag and barreling at a fast speed. There was no way he could stop now. The kid had to know that.

Why wasn't he moving!

"Move kid!" Jayson shouted.

"Dismount!" the kid ordered.

"Crap!" came the scream from Jayson as he squeezed his brakes before he came crashing into the kid and he went tumbling over the front of his handlebars and rolled along the pavement stopping short at the kid's feet.

The triumphant kid dropped his arm with the flag and pointed it at Jayson's face, "You are supposed to stop and dismount!"

Jayson jumped up from the ground, "What is your problem kid!"

To Jayson's surprise, the kid stepped forward and leaned into Jayson's body and stared him down.

Jayson stepped back, picked up his bike and walked around the kid, "I don't have time for this!"

He walked across the street and pushed his bike the rest of the way to the bike rack and locked it up.

He didn't turn around but as he walked up the steps to the front door of SOS, he saw the waving red flag reflected in the glass.

When the door closed behind him, Jayson was struck by how quiet the school was. It was only his third day, but the fifteen minutes early apparently made the world of difference.

To the left of the front door was a bulletin board with announcements pinned to them. On the top left-hand side was a reminder for the new student barbeque that was being held Saturday afternoon.

Hard pass, Jayson thought to himself.

He scanned the sheets which were mostly opportunities for students to pick up volunteer hours that were required by all students.

"You know, a lot of those slots are filling up," Miss Hanover, the school secretary popped her head above the counter that blocked her computer, and her, from view. "And, you will need to submit your placement by Monday."

"Crap, one more thing Mr. Felton can drop on me," Jayson murmured.

"Jayson, I see you made it on time today."

Jayson jumped at the sound of Mr. Felton's voice and wondered if he had complained aloud, and if he did, if Mr. Felton heard him.

"Uh, yeah," Jayson said.

Mr. Felton nodded and continued to walk past him and straight into his office. Jayson closed his eyes and breathed a sigh of relief. He turned back towards the board and found one placement that he thought he could do while remaining anonymous. Jayson yanked the flyer from the small yellow pin that held it in place and shoved it into his pocket.

Then he headed down the hall to his homeroom.

Today was the first day Jayson was walking into room 145 before either of the morning bells rang. He was, however, disappointed to see that the seat beside Jonnie was taken and the only empty desk was the one next to Goth Girl.

Even arriving early, Jayson managed to be the last one arriving to class.

Jayson and Goth Girl looked at each other briefly as he sat down and for a moment, he thought she was going to say something to him, but then she recoiled and turned her face back down to the book she was reading.

Jonnie tapped him on the shoulder with his picking hand.

"What happened at detention?" he asked.

"We had to go to detention, is what happened," Jayson said. "What do you think?"

"Who's we?"

"Me, the goon who punched me, some quiet girl and her," Jayson tilted his head back towards Goth Girl.

Jonnie's eyes widened, "Really?"

The bell rang and Jonnie slipped back into his seat as Mr. Crane walked into the room and started to take attendance.

When he reached the Rs and called Jayson's name, Jayson yelled out, "Here."

And as Mr. Crane moved on to the next kid, Jayson was sure he heard someone whisper Marshmallow from the back of the room.

CHAPTER 7

3:45 pm seemed to come slower on day three.

The benefit of the first day of high school starting on a Wednesday is that Friday comes even faster. Unfortunately, it also meant that more homework was assigned for the weekend.

Not that it mattered a whole lot to Jayson.

While murmurs of protest rang from other students in his classes because of the new student barbeque or other social engagements, Jayson knew he had nothing to do. Well, except for dinner at his aunt's house, if you can call that a social engagement. At least his aunt didn't share the same affinity for experimental cooking that his mom now did. So, there was that to look forward to.

Room 367 was on the opposite side of the school from where Jayson's last class for the day was. Goth Girl had her face buried in a book, the quiet girl was organizing her notes and Moore was sitting in a chair tipped back on two legs and had his feet perched on the top of the desk.

God, he'd love to pull that chair back.

Jayson always imagined detention being more of a dark dungeony experience. Instead, it just looked like what it was. A mostly empty classroom.

"Moore, feet off the desk," Mr. Crane said as he walked into the room.

Moore nodded and smiled and in one swift move lifted his feet off the desk and slid his chair back righting himself in the process. He flicked his hair away from the front of his face and pushed it back into its brushed-up position, and surprisingly, it held. He rested his left foot on the basketball that was on the floor next to his bag and leaned back in his seat.

Jayson hated to admit it, but even in detention, the goon knew how to look cool.

Mr. Crane placed his bag on a desk and pulled out some paper. He placed one in front of each detainee and then sat on the top of one of the desks at the front of the room. He was turned facing them with his feet on a chair and rested his forearms on his knees.

"I don't know why the four of you didn't take the option of a parent meeting to avoid this detention, but whatever the reason, here we are," Mr. Crane began. "You have one last chance to change your mind."

Mr. Crane looked back and forth from each detainee and one by one each of them shook their heads.

Jayson knew why he wasn't taking the option of a parent meeting; he couldn't figure out why the others didn't jump at the chance.

"Ok, then the purpose of your detention is to push through the message that fights, like the one that broke out in the cafeteria, will not be tolerated," Mr. Crane explained.

"*And, that we're going to be used as an example*," Jayson thought to himself.

"So," Mr. Crane continued. "Each of you is going to write an essay as to why what happened the other day is wrong."

All four began to protest in unison, but each for a different reason.

"If I miss any practices, I'll be thrown off the team!" Moore shouted, and for the first time, looked worried and vulnerable.

"I have a little brother I need to watch after school," Goth Girl said. "Unless I can bring him here?" She sneered.

Lucy, almost at a whisper said, "I have extra courses I am taking. I need that time after school!"

Not wanting to be left out, Jayson added, "I have commitments after school too." He was glad that Mr.

Crane didn't ask him to elaborate. He couldn't really use sneaking out to his fort or missing his best friend as a commitment.

Instead, Mr. Crane said, "Then what do you suggest?"

With the proverbial ball in their court, the four detainees sat quietly. All thinking about how they could easily get out of detention, on with their lives, and away from each other.

It was obvious to anyone at a quick glance that none of them had anything in common. They couldn't have picked four kids who were more unalike to serve detention for a full year together.

Then Jayson had an idea. Well, it was more like something he remembered from a show he watched, but he thought it might work.

He reached into his pocket and pulled out the crumpled sheet he grabbed off the bulletin board at beginning of the day. He flattened the sheet on the top of the desk and held it out to Mr. Crane, "What if we each do some extra community service as a way to serve detention?"

Mr. Crane stood up and walked toward Jayson and took the sheet he was holding in his outstretched hand.

"That way," Jayson said. "We don't have to miss any of our, uh, commitments and you don't have to show up and babysit us all year."

Mr. Crane nodded his head as he read the sheet and wagged his finger, "Not a bad idea." He turned around and walked back to where his bag rested on the front desk. "I know the lady who runs this program. I can make a call and get the four of you signed up."

"Oh, well, I didn't mean we had to do it *together*," Jayson said.

"No. No. It's a good idea," Mr. Crane said. "The whole idea of this detention is to have each of you work together and learn from your mistake."

"We were not fighting. We don't even know each other," Jayson assumed that the other kids were in the same position as he was.

He looked at Lucy, Moore and Goth Girl and they all nodded. His guess was right.

"See!" Jayson said.

"I still think it's a good idea," Mr. Crane said. "And since it's downtown and I am sure none of you have your license yet, why don't we coordinate going together?"

Great, Jayson thought. This just keeps getting better.

"And since this placement will require a bit of coordination and time, let's say once a week," Mr. Crane suggested. "As opposed to serving daily detention here. That way each of you can continue with your sports, homework, whatever."

Although Jayson didn't like the idea of spending volunteer placement hours with the others, he liked the idea of sitting in room 367 all year even less.

Each of them nodded in reluctant agreement.

"Then the last thing to do is to choose a day," Mr. Crane said.

Eventually, everyone agreed that Wednesday would be the best day of the week to commit to the placement. And Mr. Crane also promised Moore that he would speak to the basketball coach and ensure that he wouldn't lose his position on the team. Moore let out a sigh of relief. Jayson rolled his eyes.

Mr. Crane looked at the clock, "I think we can call it a day, guys. Why don't you head home for the weekend?"

Everyone began to gather their books and bags and stood to leave.

"Where is the placement, Mr. Crane?" Lucy asked.

"St. Agatha's Church Soup Kitchen."

They nodded. Hard to hate the idea of helping out at a soup kitchen.

As they were at the door when Mr. Crane called out, "And I'll see you all this weekend for the new student barbeque I hope?"

Nobody answered, but Jayson didn't think it was really intended as a question either.

As Jayson unlocked his bike and slipped on his helmet, he thought to himself only one hundred and ninety-four days to go.

CHAPTER 8

JayBart Followers: 11 New Likes: 1
JamToe Followers: 35 New Likes: 9
ShaneR Followers: 1211 New Likes: 83

Saturday was the one day each week that Jayson was eager to get up early. Mostly because he would normally meet up with James and they would spend the day hanging out. Now that James lived in Edmonton, the only thing Jayson had to do for the day was homework, cut the lawn and dinner at his aunt's house.

Shane left for hockey practice early and Jayson could hear him in the kitchen as he was getting ready to leave. When the house was finally quiet, Jayson jumped out of bed and headed downstairs.

He was shocked to see his mom sitting at the kitchen table reading the paper and drinking a coffee.

"Oh, hi mom," Jayson stammered. "I thought you left with Shane?"

"No, your dad took him today. I wanted to be here when you woke up and make you a special breakfast and to find out how your first week of high school was."

His mom shoved the paper to the far end of the table, pushed her chair back and walked to the counter. The bright blue mixing bowl dad gave her last Christmas was next to the oven and a spoon was resting inside of it.

Jayson wondered what creation she was planning on whipping up today.

"How are your classes?" his mom asked as she leaned into the fridge.

"Okay, I guess."

"Any kids from your last school in your classes?"

"Some."

"Anything exciting happen at school this week?"

"It's only been three days, mom."

His mom put some items on the counter and then turned to face Jayson, "I just want to make sure that everything is okay."

"Why wouldn't it be?"

"I know you were looking forward to starting high school with your best friend."

She was right about that, "Yeah, but it's okay."

His mom smiled, "Good."

She turned around and began to work away at his breakfast, whistling as she cooked.

Ten minutes later she presented Jayson with a plate of scrambled tofu egg product, sprinkled with fake cheese and meatless bacon and a side of whatever it was that she was passing off as toast nowadays.

Jayson took a sip of the juice. At least that was real.

He scarfed down breakfast as fast as he could and then rushed upstairs to get changed and start the yard work that he promised his dad he would finish.

It was an agreement he had with his dad the day he turned fifteen. If Jayson put in three hours of chores every weekend, at the end of the year his dad would buy him the small tin boat he was eyeing last summer.

It was something that he and James always said they wanted to do. Go out on the river and fish. And since neither of them had a cottage, it was a choice between one of the two rivers that intersected the city that would have to do.

When he was finished, he washed up and ran down the stairs where everyone was waiting to go to his aunt's house for dinner

His aunt was his mom's younger sister, but it was hard to tell her real age since she let her hair go grey several years ago. His mom and his aunt were polar opposites and he wondered what it was like for them growing up.

His mom, Rose, was always referred to as the pretty one and his aunt Alice was the 'other one'. Old family photos, some faded others black and white, told the story of their youth.

Jayson's mom had lighter hair than her sister, blue eyes and a petite frame. Aunt Alice, on the other hand, had a strong athletic build, dark hair and eyes, and she wore her hair cropped short through her youth.

Jayson's mom went on to law school and practiced at a large firm downtown. That is until she quit last January after Riley tried to kill herself.

Aunt Alice, on the other hand, was a gym teacher at a school downtown and volunteered at most school and sporting events that each of her three sons were involved with.

His cousins; Peter, Patrick and Paul, were a set of triplets born a year before Shane. Jayson remembered overhearing his father joke with his mom that they were an experiment gone wrong. He didn't know what his father was referring to, but as the three Ps grew older, Jayson began to realize what his father saw in their youth.

They were loud, obnoxious and rude. Even by a teenager's standard. Jayson had nothing in common with them and he hated being around them. Whenever they were at family functions Jayson, Riley and Shane clung together like a group of starfish caught in a current. Which is how they often felt around them.

But that wasn't the only reason that Jayson didn't like coming over to his aunt's house.

There was the matter of the day his grandmother died that always, eventually, reared its ugly head.

Jayson was always close to his grandmother. She was always the fun grandparent and would never shy away from playing a game with any of her grandkids. Even the three Ps didn't seem to frighten her.

His grandmother was also fiercely independent. She lived on her own until she was ninety-two which, at that point, she took a bad fall and broke her hip. After she recovered and was ready to be released from the hospital, his mom and aunt gave her the choice. She could either live with one of them or in Shady Oaks Retirement Villa.

His grandmother hated being told what to do, but at the same time, she was nervous about living alone after her fall. She chose to live with us but then after some logistics were worked out on paper, it was decided that Aunt Alice's home was a better fit.

His grandmother grew frailer and sicker as the years passed and last June it became clear that she didn't have long to live. Jayson spent most of his free time with his grandmother. He would either read to her, sneak her in snacks, or just sit and watch television with her as she drifted in and out of sleep.

On the day she died Jayson was sitting alone with her in her room. He could see her drifting away, but he didn't call anyone into the room. She looked so peaceful and happy that he didn't want to ruin it for her.

His grandmother reached out her arm and Jayson took hold of it.

"Yes, Nana?" he said. "I'm right here."

Her hand felt light, cold and boney in his grip. He leaned over her bed and she waved him in closer. And when his face was just over hers, she whispered a secret that she had been keeping her whole life and was finally ready to tell.

She fell silent after she spoke and just at the same moment his aunt walked into the room.

Ever since then, his aunt has been pestering Jayson to tell her what his grandmother said. And there was no way he could ever tell her. He couldn't tell anyone. He wasn't even sure why his grandmother told him.

What a crappy thing to lay on your grandkid. No matter how much he loved his grandmother, it was a shitty thing to have done to him.

He had avoided his aunt for most of the day. Since the three Ps could barely sit still, meals were set as a buffet and you piled your plates high with food and then found a place to plop down and eat.

Shane, Riley and Jayson found a quiet corner at the far end of the back deck and inhaled the food on their plates. Without speaking, he and his brother and sister munched down on the barbeque steak, whipped mashed potatoes (with real bacon) and butter-laden garlic bread (real bread) with excruciating joy.

They didn't know when they would get a meal like this again.

Out of the corner of his eye, Jayson could see his aunt approaching them. Balancing three pieces of cake, she wove her way around the three Ps that were sitting on the other side of the deck.

Jayson, Riley and Shane eagerly grabbed a plate and began to dig into the creamy strawberry filling, digging it out of the center of the layers of cake.

His aunt wiggled her body between Jayson and Shane until Shane almost fell off the end of the bench.

Riley nodded towards the lawn, "Come on, Shane. Let's go sit on the swing."

The two of them ran off towards the far end of the lawn leaving Jayson to fend for himself, and alone with his aunt.

"How was your dinner, Jayson?"

"Good thanks," Jayson kept spooning cake into his mouth, hoping it would keep her from asking her standard question.

"I know my sister Rose has got you all on some crazy diet," his aunt said, waving her hand in the air like she was shooing a fly away.

"It's not so bad," Jayson lied.

"You know who a good cook was?" his aunt asked. "Your grandmother."

And there it was.

He had to hand it to his aunt, she was getting faster at segueing into talking about the day his grandmother died.

"Yep," was all Jayson said.

His aunt slapped her hand on her lap, "Why won't you just tell us?"

Jayson leaned his head forward and closer to the plate, trying to ignore her and shoveling the last of the cake into his mouth.

"Jayson, I have a right to know what she said to you!" his aunt yelled.

"She didn't say anything!" Jayson snapped. "Stop asking."

"I saw her whisper something to you," his aunt demanded, pointing a stubby finger in his face. "Do you know how selfish you're being?"

“Do you know how crazy you’re being?” Jayson’s inner voice sprang forward, and he regretted the words as they left his mouth.

“Come on Jayson, we have to leave,” his mother was suddenly standing in front of him and glaring at his aunt.

Her sister.

The other one.

And he could tell by the look in his aunt’s eyes that she wasn’t going to let it go.

CHAPTER 9

JayBart Followers: 11 New Likes: 0
JamToe Followers: 40 New Likes: 5
ShaneR Followers: 1217 New Likes: 65

Since January attending church became mandatory for the Routledges. Finding Riley on the floor of the bathroom sent his parents into a fit of prayer. His mom must have made some huge deal with God because as soon as Riley came home from the hospital, they have attended church every Sunday since then.

Shane even got into the excitement of it all. Truth be told, he was focusing on applying to a high school that was known for its hockey program and, surprise surprise, it happened to be Catholic. He was upping his chances of getting accepted by getting involved with our church, and today, that meant watching Shane take his first steps in being an altar boy. Jayson had to hand it to Shane. When he did something, he rarely went halfway.

Shane sauntered through the church before mass waving at a few of his friends (there for the same reason) and making sure that the principal of the Catholic high school got a clear view of who he was. Jayson watched him and thought he was one step away from drama school and then a few more from Hollywood as he commanded the role with ease. He even convinced his mother to buy him a pair of red shoes to complete the look. Jayson wasn't sure his mother saw the connection to the fact that the Pope's shoes were red as well.

Father Monahan finished his sermon and when mass was over everyone filed down to the basement for donuts and coffee. Jayson and Riley begged to be excused, but his mom insisted.

"Father Monahan was very kind after you came home from the hospital, Riley. It's the least we could do."

Jayson could see his sister cringe at the mention of her return from the hospital, sure that it was eliciting painful memories of her suicide attempt.

Jayson followed Riley as she stormed off ahead of their parents and froze when he caught sight of Mr. Crane.

"Oh, crap!" Jayson said.

Riley turned around to see what Jayson was talking about, "What is it?"

"My teacher, Mr. Crane," Jayson pointed across the room. "I can't let him talk to mom and dad."

"Why?"

"You know that fight in the cafeteria?"

"The one where you got the bruise?"

"Yeah. That one. Well, I also got a year's detention along with it," Jayson confessed.

"No shit," his sister laughed.

"Yeah, and I don't want mom and dad to find out."

Riley grabbed Jayson's shoulder and began to pull him towards the door. But just as Jayson and Riley were turning to leave, Mr. Crane called out his name, "Jayson!"

He strolled over towards where they were standing, his parents a short distance away.

"I didn't know you were a member of this church," Mr. Crane said.

"Yeah, well I am," Jayson rambled out quickly. "Gotta go. Bye."

"Jayson, is this one of your teachers?" his mom asked as she walked up behind them.

Crap, Jayson thought.

"Uh, yeah. Mom, Dad, this is Mr. Crane," Jayson made the introduction, hoping it would end there. He looked to Riley for help, but she just stood watching his life unfold.

"Nice to meet you both," Mr. Crane shook both my parent's hands. "I guess we would have eventually met up at parent-teacher night."

They still do those in high school?

"I am excited to work with Jayson this year at St. Agatha's," Mr. Crane said.

Here it comes, Jayson thought. At least he was in a church, how badly could his parents yell at him while they were standing in front of a twelve-foot crucifix.

"What's going on at St. Agatha's?" his father asked.

Mr. Crane looked at Jayson and then back at his parents, "Jayson didn't tell you? It was his idea."

Jayson squeezed his eyes closed and lowered his face.

"Jayson and three other students are going to be working with me once a week at a soup kitchen that is run out of St. Agatha's."

"Really!" his parents both said in unison.

"Really?" Riley asked.

"Really," Jayson confirmed.

After a few seconds of awkward silence, Mr. Crane said it was nice to meet his parents and said goodbye, "See you Monday, Jayson."

Jayson lifted his hand a few inches above his belt and gave a feeble wave to his teacher. And with his mother thinking he made three new friends and Riley still waiting for a full explanation, they joined Shane in the basement before finally heading home.

CHAPTER 10

JayBart Followers: 11 New Likes: 2
JamToe Followers: 43 New Likes: 13
ShaneR Followers: 1218 New Likes: 69

The high school class timetable was different than it was up to grade eight. Classes cycled through a six-day schedule and during that time Jayson had gym class three times. Today was day four in the schedule and his first day of gym class in high school.

Even though he had slimmed out since grade school, Jayson never took easily to sports. He was always slightly awkward and except for riding his bike or skateboarding, he had little interest in participating in sports. Probably because he preferred to just do things by himself or with James, who wasn't around anymore anyway.

Kids were free to wear their own shorts and t-shirts for class, but everyone had to make sure they had actual running shoes. Not boarding shoes or slip-ons, but real actual running shoes.

Student lockers were assigned alphabetically, and Jayson's was on the main floor next to the gym. He tossed his backpack into his locker and then grabbed the small orange bag with his shoes and shorts. He hovered over his lock, spinning the dial waiting for most of the kids to leave the locker room before he went inside.

He spotted Moore at the end of the hall. He was leaning on his locker, his left hand tucked into his jacket pocket and his right hand slipped around a girl's waist.

Jayson recognized the girl as MaryBeth McGuire. Not Mary. Not Beth. But MaryBeth.

She was in class with Jayson from grade four when her family moved to the city, right up until the end of grade eight. She wasn't in any of his classes so far at SOS, and for that he was grateful.

MaryBeth was the kind of person that knew everything, including how to get other people to do things for her. She always managed to get out of extra class duties, and she was even able to convince Mr. Hoilstein that the required long distance runs in gym class were dangerous for her ankles.

Somehow, however, MaryBeth received one of the highest grades in gym class.

MaryBeth took off down the hall when she realized she was late for practice, leaving Moore alone at his locker. Her pleated skirt and maroon knit sweater gave away the fact that she was on the SOS cheerleading team. Jayson guessed her ankles had improved somewhat.

Jayson spun his lock closed and hurried off to get changed for gym class.

He walked into the gym and the sound of balls bouncing off the basketball backboards and the squeak of rubber on the polished gym floor echoed in the cavernous space.

"Jayson!" Jonnie yelled from the far end of the gym.

Jayson turned to answer him, and a ball came flying into the side of his face. He stumbled backward before eventually falling into the pile of balls that were laying on the floor.

Under the sound of laughter Jayson could hear Jonnie running over to him, "Oh, man, you okay?"

"Yeah," Jayson jumped up before anyone else saw him laying on the floor, having been taken out by a twenty-two-ounce ball.

Jayson dragged his hand across the top of his lip and was glad to see there wasn't a trail of blood.

A loud sharp whistle blew from the center of the room.

"Okay group, pair off into twos and start your push-ups!"

"Isn't that what pairing off means?" Jayson asked. "Groups of two."

"Ha! Yeah!" Jonnie laughed.

Jonnie and Jayson had an understanding, apparently, that they would both partner up in classes whenever it was required for projects or assignments. Jayson didn't see any point in trying to get away from him since there was no one that Jayson had to get away to. And for all the annoying habits Jonnie had, he had never been unkind to Jayson. Or to anyone else for that matter.

After the class completed a session of forced reps of squats and push-ups to chants of 'go hard or go home', they were split off into two groups. One team was given red pinneys to slip over their shirts and all were told they were going to play a quick game of basketball.

Now, Jayson normally didn't shy away from pick-up games that they were forced to play in gym. But they were in a different league now! He was going to have to go up against both guys and girls who were playing on high level competitive leagues.

"Looks like the other team is stacked," Jayson growled so only Jonnie could hear him.

On the other side of the gym Moore and his group of goons were slipping red pinneys over their t-shirts and high fiving each other before they began.

"Does anyone even high five anymore?" Jonnie asked Jayson.

Jayson smiled. Just what he was thinking. Like it was even necessary to pump each other up. It was clear by looking at the collection of faded, thin and out of shape students on Jayson's side of the gym that they were going to get creamed.

The first quarter ended with a 29 to 2 score. No need to guess which side Jayson and Jonnie were on.

The second quarter went much the same way and the half-time split saw most of Jayson's team draped over the small bench begging for an end to the slaughter. Heavy breathing and students clutching their sides made the red-faced sweaty group look more pathetic on the bench than they were on the court.

The whistle blew and Jayson was on the next shift called up.

Jayson wasn't sure how, but at one point the ball ended up clutched in the middle of his hands, and astonishingly he was standing alone on one end of the court. He wasn't enough of an athletic threat to be guarded by the other players, but they didn't hesitate as they now charged towards him.

"Oh, crap!" Jayson yelled as he watched what seemed like half of the competitive basketball team come straight at him. He panicked and then rushed to dribble the ball towards the opposite net. He bounced the ball alongside each stride he took as he headed towards the net. Occasionally looking behind hoping by some small miracle that he may outrun someone from the other team. After all, he did go to church last Sunday and he did say a few convincing prayers.

Just as Jayson was getting ready to release the ball into the air, and to fate, he prayed it would land somewhere close to the rim. A fist landed in the center of his back and someone's foot hooked his right ankle.

With little warning, Jayson came crashing to the floor and then with the force of his speed he skidded across the floor feeling the skin on his knees burn until he finally came to a stop under the net.

He watched as the ball teetered on the edge of the rim and then finally, in slow motion, toilet spun through the middle of the net and then landed on his face.

His vision cleared with the sound of his motley teammates cheering the success of his three-point basket. Jayson smiled, the swelling on his forehead was going to be worth the basket. He saw a hand reach out to help him up and he grabbed it. It wasn't until he was standing, he realized it was Moore who helped him off the floor.

"Good basket," Moore said before running back to where his team congregated on their bench.

Jayson rejoined his team and watched the remainder of the game (which they lost miserably) with an ice pack pushed against the front of his head.

The whole way home Jayson couldn't wait to send James the picture he took of his team as they were sitting on the bench.

Jayson rolled his bike alongside the side of the garage and ran into the house, yelling hello to his mother as he passed her on the stairs.

He could hear her whistling as he ran into his room and closed the door. He tossed his bag on the floor and jumped on his bed, landing on his back. He pulled out his phone and opened his app.

He uploaded the image of the red, sweaty and bruised group that got hammered in their basketball game in gym class today and added #basketball #sos #highschool and pressed 'post'.

He scrolled through his profile and was even shocked to see he gained two more followers. He now sat at thirteen, not as many as Shane, but it's moving in the right direction.

A photo of James giving a thumbs up at a burger joint crawled through his feed and Jayson quickly liked it. A couple more pictures on James' profile showed him riding along a riverbank with three other guys with the hashtags #friends #edmonton #saskriver.

Jayson froze on the picture for a few seconds before liking it. It wasn't the picture or the hashtags that threw Jayson for a loop it was the fact that James was wearing an Edmonton Oiler's sweatshirt.

Then he saw it. On the top of James' profile, he had not only changed his picture from the one of him and Jayson sitting in their fort to one of him alone, but he changed his profile name.

He was no longer JamToe but JamesT42.

Jayson reached for the pillow on his bed and held it against his face and screamed.

CHAPTER 11

It was two days since Jayson tried to text James and he still hadn't heard from him. But then James never tried to text Jayson either. The last few times they did text, their conversation didn't last for longer than a few lines back and forth and Jayson didn't have the courage to ask him why he changed his profile picture and name. The ones they picked for each other because they were best friends.

It was Wednesday and the first day of the detention group's volunteer stint at St. Agatha's Soup Kitchen. At least Jayson hoped he could find a space to keep to himself while he was there. Jayson had been there once with his mom and he remembered it was the kind of place that you could be given a chore that you could do yourself. Like wash the dishes, set out some plates and even wipe the tables.

Jayson waited in the parking lot for Mr. Crane and the others to arrive. Mr. Crane had a large white van, the kind you were told to avoid as a kid, and it was used to mostly shuttle the school's sports teams to and from games around the city.

Mr. Crane arrived at the same time as Lucy, Moore and Goth Girl and they all piled into the van and were on their way.

The van's three bench seats gave everyone a zone where they could avoid each other. Moore took the seat furthest in the back, Jayson sat in the bench seat directly in front of him and Lucy and Goth Girl sat in the bench behind Mr. Crane but with space between them.

The drive downtown took less than twenty-five minutes and Mr. Crane spoke the entire time. Filling the awkward silence with instructions on what they should say, how they should listen and, of course, what not to say or do.

You'd think he believed they had never been taken out in public before today.

They arrived at St. Agatha's a little after four and just in time to prepare for the dinner rush. The basement of the church hall was converted into a soup kitchen with the use of donations from local businesses and parishioners. Three elderly women were working in the kitchen and Jayson could hear their laughter as they worked alongside each other cutting and assembling food on trays.

"Ernie!" a woman with shiny silver hair cut in a bob style walked towards them. She wiped her hands on her apron, stained with food from many meals she prepared at St. Agatha's. She smiled as she wrapped her arms around Mr. Crane.

"Kids, this is my mom," Mr. Crane announced and then proceeded to introduce each kid individually.

"Well, I'm just so glad that you are all here to help today. We really need it," the elder Mrs. Crane said. "I'll get you to all put on aprons and hairnets and then we'll get started."

They walked over to the table just inside the kitchen and they each grabbed a folded apron and a bag with a hair net inside.

With some fumbling, they managed to wrap the apron around their necks and then secure them with the straps around their waist. Goth Girl had the hardest time with the hairnet and Mrs. Crane had to help her tuck her waist length hair inside.

"Now, I'll get you to line up behind the table and as our patrons come in, I want you to serve them from your tray," she guided them along the table. "One scoop per person. And they can always come back for seconds."

"I can help in the back if you want?" Jayson asked.

"That's okay. We need you out here."

Mrs. Crane left them to find their place and get comfortable before her son, their teacher, Ernie Crane, opened the doors. People started coming in. Slowly at first but then eventually there was a line at the table that extended to the door.

Jayson wasn't sure what to expect from the people that came into the soup kitchen. He just could recall images he saw online of homeless people but realizing that never once did he see a story from their perspective. Each scoop of mashed potatoes that Jayson piled on each plate was met with a smile, a nod, or a thank you. There wasn't a mad rush towards the table nor were there any rude demands. Why did he think there would be anyway?

He could tell the others were probably thinking the same thing. He was standing beside Moore who was handing out slices of bread. Each one he grabbed with a pair of stainless-steel prongs and placed them on the edge of each plate. Each time he smiled and said the same thing.

"Enjoy."

How could this be the same guy who sucker punched him in the cafeteria and got them all into trouble?

The crowd started to thin out and the line slowed down as people were eating. Lucy and Goth Girl had started talking about something, but Jayson had no clue as to what they would have in common, and he and Moore were just standing beside each other staring down at their dwindling supply of mashed potatoes and bread.

"Hey, how's about an extra scoop?" came the plea from a short man with a toothless grin who beamed a hopeful stare at Jayson.

"I'm not supposed to," Jayson said. "But you can come back for seconds."

"Awe, that's no good," the old man smiled. "I've got a bum knee. Ask anyone about it." The man introduced himself as Pesky Pete, and Jayson thought that if he didn't give him an extra scoop of potatoes that he would live up to his name. He smiled at Jayson and then proceeded to pursue an extra slice of bread from Moore with the same line he just used with Jayson.

"So that was a pretty cool shot you took in gym the other day," Moore said out of nowhere.

"Uh, yeah," Jayson said. "A total fluke."

"Yeah, I thought so," Moore said. But there was something in the way he said it that made them both laugh - and Jayson not feel insulted.

Lucy and Goth Girl looked at them, perplexed that they had found something to laugh at in a soup kitchen, not realizing that they were both laughing at Jayson.

"Sssh," Lucy hushed them, holding her finger over her lips.

Jayson mouthed the word 'sorry' and returned to his tray of mashed potatoes and moved them around.

"Hey, I saw you brought your skateboard to school today," Moore said.

"Yeah, I thought I would get in as much as I could before the snow comes," Jayson said.

"Ever use a longboard?" Moore asked.

"Once," Jayson answered. "But no surprise I ended up flat on my face."

They both laughed, this time much quieter.

"Hey, it was pretty cool that you came up with the idea that we do this," Moore said. "It got us out of that detention room for the rest of the year."

"And, we get to use our hours here for volunteering too," Jayson added.

"Smart," Moore said. "I hadn't thought of that. That'll be good because I'm pretty busy with sports after school and on weekends."

"Yeah," Jayson stopped short of saying 'me too'. He just wasn't busy doing anything really.

"Okay kids," Mr. Crane walked along the front of their table. "Time to go. Why don't you hand off your spoons to the next shift, toss your aprons in the bin and meet me outside and I'll get you home."

When they returned to the van, their awkwardness with each other returned and they sat in the spaced-out seating pattern they did on the way down to the soup kitchen.

Everyone except Lucy pulled out their phones and were zoned out for the entire drive. Even Mr. Crane had found little more to say to the group.

"You can drop me at the school Mr. Crane," Goth Girl said.

"Me too," Lucy added. "My dad's picking me up there."

Moore and Jayson also agreed they could be dropped at the school.

Except for Lucy's dad's SUV, the parking lot was empty when they arrived. Lucy jumped out of the van and waved at the group, "Bye".

Goth Girl slid across the seat and mumbled something that Jayson assumed was a farewell and began to walk across the front lawn of SOS before she disappeared around the corner. Jayson and Moore crawled out from the back of the van and then nodded at each other before going their separate ways.

Jayson was only a few steps away from the van when he heard his name being called by Mr. Crane.

"It was nice to meet your parents, Jayson," Mr. Crane said. "And I'm assuming that the way the conversation went that they don't know about the detention or the fight."

Jayson shook his head, "And I'd prefer to keep it that way if it's all the same to you."

Mr. Crane tucked both his hands in the front pocket of his jeans, slipping his thumbs through his belt loops, "No problem. And for what it's worth, I think it was a great idea that you had to get the others to get on board with the soup kitchen."

Well, you did that, but okay, Jayson thought, I'll take the credit.

Mr. Crane nodded his head and said goodbye before heading back into the school.

Jayson watched as Mr. Crane left the parking lot area and ran up the steps of the school. He didn't think a teacher could be likable, and Mr. Crane was getting alarmingly close to being almost cool.

Jayson dropped his skateboard to the ground and jumped on it. With a quick push, he pulled the straps of his backpack tighter and weaved his way down the slight incline of the lot picking up speed as he went.

He saw Moore walking up ahead and was about to call out his name, but he noticed he was deep in conversation with another kid and decided against it.

A chill was blowing in the air and Jayson zipped up the front of his fleece, jumped the curb and headed home.

But Jayson couldn't shake the feeling he knew the kid from somewhere.

CHAPTER 12

Wednesdays turned out to be a day of the week that Jayson looked forward to. It was a routine that he could count on and there were no surprises to worry about. It had been more than a month that they were coming to St. Agatha's and working the crowd, which is how Jayson would describe his volunteer sessions.

They learned to recognize the regulars as well as their likes and dislikes. Pesky Pete was one of Jayson's favorites and when he would hold out his plate, Jayson would scoop an extra serving of mashed potatoes, saving him a trip back for seconds.

There was no one that any of them said they disliked, but they did learn to approach Bethany with caution. She would sometimes come in and behave in a calm and orderly fashion, but there were moments when she would blast through the door and start accusing them of putting something in the food.

"I know you're trying to control my mind with that stuff," she would blurt out, unfortunately to Lucy who just stared at her with fright.

"No, really, they're just green beans with a little butter," Lucy would respond trying to soothe Bethany and coax her into taking some food.

Bethany would ultimately recoil and point two fingers in Lucy's direction, apparently her way of warding off the effects of the tainted beans.

Mrs. Crane caught sight of Bethany that day and came up and placed her hand on Lucy's shoulders, "Don't take it personally Lucy. Some of our patrons are sick and they sometimes may seem confused. Just be there with the offer of food. If they take it, they take it."

"But if she's sick, why doesn't she get help?" Lucy asked.

To which Mrs. Crane responded, "It's not always that simple Lucy."

Later the group came to realize that the service that St. Agatha provided went beyond the food. They offered a safe place to come to, without judgment and without pressure.

When the meal service ended, the four offered to stay and help clean up as they waited for Mr. Crane who had texted and said he would be delayed.

Moore and Jayson were sitting on the floor near the door laughing when Goth Girl and Lucy walked over. Goth Girl leaned against the wall and slid her tall thin body down until she was sitting facing the two boys.

"What are you two giggling about?" she asked.

"Laughing, not giggling," Jayson corrected her.

"Just some skateboard fails," Moore said as he turned his phone to face Goth Girl and Lucy, who was now sitting next to her.

Lucy let out a loud 'OMG laugh' as she slapped her hand over her mouth and Goth Girl tried to fight a smile but it, along with a laugh, ultimately emerged.

"Do you follow the GoonSquad45 profile?" Goth Girl asked.

Moore turned his phone around and began typing the profile name into his search bar, "No, what is it?"

"These guys that go around the city doing those crazy building jumping stunts," Goth Girl pounded her palm against her forehead. "Oh, what's that called again!"

"Parkour," Jayson said.

Goth Girl pointed her blackened fingertip at him, "That's it!"

She then turned to Lucy, "Hey, what's your profile?"

Lucy's eyes darted from Goth Girl's to Jayson's and Moore's and then rested on her lap. She twisted her fingers together, "I don't have one."

"What!" Moore asked. "Why?'

"My parents won't let me," Lucy said.

"Why not?" Goth Girl asked. "Did you get in trouble by posting some bad stuff?"

Jayson was sure this wasn't the reason.

"No. They're just super strict."

"What *are* you allowed to do?" Jayson asked.

"Jayson?" Goth Girl snapped.

"No. That's okay. I don't mind," Lucy said. "They are not originally from Canada. We moved here when I was a baby and my two younger sisters were born after we arrived. They love Canada and our life here and all the opportunity for me and my sisters, but they still believe a lot of what they learned growing up in India is still of value when raising a family."

"Like?" this time it was Moore who asked the question, but Jayson noticed that Goth Girl didn't reprimand him.

"Like, they believe in technology, of course, but not for the useless banter that is on most of the social media sites. Their main focus is for me to finish with top grades so I can get accepted into whatever University or program I am interested in, anywhere in the world."

"That's a lot of pressure," Jayson said.

"Well, they made it to Canada, didn't they?" Lucy countered. "It's just who they are."

"You can do both you know Lucy?" Moore said.

Lucy nodded her head from side to side and whispered, "Maybe."

Goth Girl sensed that Lucy was feeling uncomfortable and changed the focus of the conversation towards Moore and Jayson.

"Quick, what are your profiles?"

"MattMoore," Moore said.

Of course, his was just his name. No numbers or symbols were needed, *and* it was available. Did his parents apply for it the day he was born?

"Jayson?" Goth Girl asked, her fingers perched on her screen.

Jayson waved his hand, "I hardly am ever on it. . ."

Goth Girl tilted her head to her shoulder, "So, you can start with us."

Why was she being so normal?

"JayBart," he said. He waited for the ridicule, but it didn't come. Instead, both Moore and Goth Girl just began to type it into their phone.

The large steel door creaked as Mr. Crane pulled it open, "Sorry I'm late guys."

Everyone grabbed their bags off the floor and ran out to the van. Jayson could feel his phone buzz from deep inside his pocket and he fought the urge to pull it out and look. If it was one of those heart emojis from his mom telling him she hoped that he was having a good day, he would just be embarrassed.

But what if it was James? He realized he hadn't spoken to him for quite a while and was eager to repair the rift in their friendship.

They piled into the van and because it was late, Mr. Crane insisted on dropping each kid at their homes and when they reached Jayson's house, Jayson yanked open the door of the van and then jumped out onto the lawn.

"Thanks for the ride," Jayson yelled as he ran towards the front door.

He kicked off his shoes and took the stairs two at a time until he reached the top. Out of breath he tossed his bag on the floor and shut his door.

He pulled his phone out of his pocket and unlocked it with his thumbprint. There was no message from James. But there was an alert on his phone. He had three new likes and one new follow. All from 'SadWill'. Goth Girl.

CHAPTER 13

JayBart Followers: 14 New Likes: 3
SadWill Followers: 21 New Likes: 4

SadWill's profile was filled with artistic photos from around the city. Areas he recognized and some he didn't. Each one, however, made him look at his city differently. Not one photo she posted had a person in them. They were aloof (which means they were kind of indifferent to the person taking them). It's what his dad called Aunt Alice, but Jayson didn't think his dad understood the definition because she always seemed so outgoing and in your face.

The other thing that struck Jayson was, that like him, she never included text, only hashtags.

He scrolled through his phone as he scooped Cheerios into his mouth. His mom finally caved and bought a box at the grocery store when his dad begged for some 'real food'.

Jayson didn't think this is what his dad had in mind, but he was happy to reap the rewards of his dad's begging.

"Put your phone away," his mom scolded him as she walked into the kitchen. "You know the rule."

Jayson turned his phone over and lowered it to the table. He pulled his bowl in close to his body, "Sorry, mom. No one was here so I thought I would just catch up."

"Hmm," his mom watched him. "You know, it's okay to put that thing down once and a while."

"I know."

His mom looked at the time, "Aren't you going to be late?"

"No school today," Jayson said as he slurped up his cereal. "PD day or something."

His mom let out a sigh. She always complained about how many days off the kids had right at the beginning of school. She would say it was hard to get into a routine if the school couldn't stick to one. But Jayson didn't mind.

"I hope you're going to get some homework done before you decide to 'relax'?" His mom wiggled her fingers in the air to signal her mocking of the word relax.

"Yes," Jayson said in a subdued tone, demoralized at the sound of homework.

Jayson finished his cereal and drank the last of the milk in the bowl, enjoying every last taste, unsure of when 'real food' would return.

He ran upstairs after he was done eating. He knew his mom would be trolling the upper floor in hopes of catching him lounging on his bed, so he decided to spend the morning completing the assignments that his teachers gave them for their extended weekend.

To Jayson's surprise, and pleasure, his grades were tracking in the high B range and he felt that he actually knew what the teachers were doing. When he was finished, he put his books in his bag and zippered it shut and tossed it on the floor by his desk where it would remain until Monday morning.

Jayson flopped on his bed and grabbed his phone.

Still no response from James.

He thought he would send him a text taunting him that he had an extra-long weekend. That should get him going.

JAYSON:
hey, 2 days off!!!
what u doing?

To Jayson's surprise a bubble quickly appeared, and three dots rolled back and forth across his screen.

JAMES:
cool
been on a school trip, camping in jasper

James then sent a picture of him and three guys, huddled around a fire. Each holding a peace sign to the camera and arms around each other. Like a band of brothers. Like he and James were before he left.

Jayson looked closer and saw that the three guys appeared in most of James' last few pictures.

His new crew.

Jayson's replacements.

Jayson then scrolled to the top of James' profile, "Holy crap!" he shouted.

James now had 792 followers.

He flopped his arms out wide and tossed his phone on his bed. He didn't realize how dejected he would feel.

Watching James have so much fun without him, traveling to so many neat spots in Alberta was bad enough. But to see he had almost eight hundred followers and he just moved to the city was too much!

Jayson grabbed his phone again. He didn't want James to think he was a poor sport, so he added. . .

JAYSON:
cool

JAMES:
what u doing with your day off?

Jayson waited, trying to think of what to say. He never thought he would need to impress James, yet that's exactly what he was feeling now. He began to type, and he knew as the words came that it was a stupid idea. But he did it anyway.

JAYSON:
got a gf
hanging out

JAMES:
WTF?!
NW

JAYSON:
yep
gtg ttyl

JAMES:
kk

Jayson was nowhere near close to having a girlfriend. The only two girls that even spoke to him were the two forced into detention with him. Jayson sighed, slipped his phone back into his pocket and left his room. Maybe he could find a snack downstairs that was semi-edible.

He walked past his sister's room and the door was open, a rare instance. Riley wasn't inside, which also was rare. He stuck his head into her room and looked around.

She had the blinds partially drawn but there were still bright beams of light streaming through the window. Her room had been her oasis for the last ten months and she had it set up more like an apartment than a bedroom.

Jayson hadn't been in Riley's room since he was in grade six or seven. She strictly forbade (and that was the word she'd used) either he or Shane to go into her room without permission. After her suicide attempt, they just did everything they could to not upset her.

Jayson stepped inside, lured by the mystery around the things that girls kept in their rooms.

For the most part, the room was not unlike his. She had books, pictures and awards (more than he had but less than Shane) on her shelves. Her desk was cluttered with papers and her writing journal, which she started after she got home from the hospital. A suggestion from Dr. Sparrow on how to deal with her anxiety.

There was one shelf that had a stack of paper that Jayson didn't remember ever seeing before. He stepped closer and looked on the shelf. Sketches and drawings were piled on top of more sketches and drawings. Each one more intricate than the one before.

Jayson reached for the sheet on the top of the pile.

"What are you doing in here?" Riley grabbed the sheet of paper out of Jayson's hand.

"I have the day off school," he said.

"That explains why you're home," she pointed out. "What are you doing in my room?"

"Sorry, I just thought I would come in and see if you were here?" He lied.

Riley tossed the sheet back on the pile, "Where else would I be?"

She turned around and walked to her bed and flopped down on the mattress.

Jayson leaned against her desk and crossed his arms and looked at her.

"What are you staring at?" Riley asked.

"Why?" Jayson asked.

"Why, what?" she asked confused.

"Why'd you do it? You know, take the pills?" Jayson blurted out, but she didn't seem surprised or upset.

She shrugged her shoulders, "It took you long enough to ask."

"I didn't want to upset you," Jayson said. "Mom and dad said we should give you your space."

"Well, thanks, but I think I have had all the space I can handle," she folded her hand in her lap and contemplated her next response. "It was stupid. I know that now. But, at the time I didn't know how else to deal with everything. I didn't see any way out of things."

Jayson wanted to sit down beside her, but he also didn't want to distract her from speaking. She was finally opening up to him.

"I didn't know you were feeling so stressed, Ry."

She nodded, "Neither did I until it was too late."

"But what were you stressed about?" It was a fair question. They lived in a good home, she had amazing grades, lots of friends and she was in a top program at the University.

"Most of it I put on myself. I never really wanted to go into Engineering. I did it because it was a challenge and when I was the first in my group of friends to get accepted, I didn't want to turn it down. And mom and dad were so proud, they wouldn't shut up about it. The program is super stressful, plus I really didn't like it,"

Riley let out a small laugh. "Then, Derek broke up with me just as exams were beginning and he was posting all these pictures of him and his new girlfriends all over the place and all my friends were liking them. It was driving me crazy. I was so busy with school and stressing about my marks, and all my friends were posting crazy pictures about all these amazing things they were doing, and I just felt like I was getting left behind. I felt like I was getting pulled under. I was missing parties; concerts and every little bit of my life was filled with what I was expected to do and not what I wanted to do."

"What do you want to do?" Jayson asked.

"Do you know you are one of the only people that has asked me that? Besides Dr. Sparrow, that is," Riley nodded at the pile of pages that were on the shelf behind Jayson.

Jayson looked at the sketches and took the same sheet that she had just taken from him and held it in his hands.

"This is great, Ry," Jayson said.

"Thanks," his sister let out a deep breath. "It feels good to show them to someone."

For the next hour, Riley showed Jayson all the sketches she drew since she was home from the hospital. The first ones were dark and edgy but as the months passed and she began to open up in her therapy sessions and started to heal they became softer and more expressive.

"What are you going to do with them?" Jayson asked.

"I don't know," Riley placed the pile of drawings back on the shelf. "I was thinking of applying to the Banff School of Fine Arts."

"Do it," Jayson demanded. "You are too good not to." Even though he had never heard of the Banff School of Fine Arts, it sounded impressive.

Riley smiled. It was one of the rare times he remembered seeing her smile since the day she swallowed the pills.

"Okay," Riley sat down on the bed next to Jayson. "Now you tell me why is it that Aunt Alice keeps harassing you about what grandma said before she died?"

"Not you too?" Jayson buried his face in his hands.

"Really," Riley said. "It's obviously bothering you. What is it about what grandma said that is so bad that you won't tell anyone?"

Jayson thought for a moment but then he realized if Riley could share something as personal as she just did, he should be able to tell her about what their grandmother said right before she died.

"I was sitting beside nana reading her some articles out of those trashy magazines Aunt Alice always has laying around," Jayson began. "She started to make a gurgling noise and I leaned in to see if she was okay and all. That's when she pulled me close and told me. And if what she said is true, it could really hurt people. People we care about," Jayson explained. "And I'm not sure what to do."

Riley thought about it for a moment, "Would it hurt mom and Aunt Alice or just Aunt Alice?"

"Does it matter?" Jayson asked.

"Yeah. Because if it won't hurt mom you may want to confide in her and tell her. But it really is up to you," Riley said. "Grandma told you and nobody else, so I guess it's your decision."

"That's not a lot of help."

They both laughed.

Riley grabbed Jayson's hand with both of hers and said, "No matter what I've got your back, Jayson."

"Me too," he said. "So, if you're ever feeling pulled under or whatever, you can always count on me."

CHAPTER 14

Today was a good day.

Up five followers, didn't have to take Shane to school and watch half his grade fawn over his arrival and Jayson was able to thwart the crossing guard bandit while he was busy harassing two kids who dared to cross before the flag was lowered.

Jayson rolled up to the base of the school steps and tapped the end of his board with his foot and then grabbed the front wheels. He made a mental note to come back to the school after everyone had left to try some jumps off the front steps.

Lockers lined the two main halls of the school. One on the main floor and the second in the basement. Jayson's locker was on the main floor close to the gym, but on the opposite side of the school where his homeroom class was. Jayson spun the dials until the combination released the lock and he gave it a hard pull, echoing the clanging of the steel on steel through the near empty hall.

“Did that lock do something to you?” Moore laughed. He was standing in front of his locker which was somewhere between the art class and Jayson’s locker.

Jayson nodded and smiled, “Yeah, I know.”

Yeah, I know? What kind of idiot response was that?

But Moore didn’t seem to notice.

Jayson thought he would try again, “Hey, who was that kid you met after soup kitchen last Wednesday?’ I thought I recognized him.”

Moore was digging around in his locker when he answered, “Just a guy I know from basketball camp. You wouldn’t know him.”

Jayson dropped his skateboard in the bottom of his locker and grabbed his copy of *To Kill A Mockingbird* from the top shelf, “He just looked familiar, that’s all.”

“I just meant that I didn’t think you’d know him,” Moore explained. He closed his locker door and for the first time since he arrived, Jayson got a clear look at his face.

“What happened to you?” Jayson said referencing the bruise on the side of Moore’s face.

Moore raised his hand to cover his cheekbone, “Oh, nothing. Just an elbow in practice.” Moore clicked his lock through the latch and spun the combination dial. “See ya,” he shouted as he ran ahead to catch up to a couple of friends. The same two buddies that had escaped detention at the beginning of the year.

The hall was beginning to fill with students loading and unloading their backpacks in their lockers and then rushing to their morning classes. Homeroom class was not quite full and there were a few seats for Jayson to choose from, but he took the same seat he had been sitting in since the first day of school. The one beside Goth Girl.

"Hey," Jayson said as Goth Girl turned her head when he arrived.

"Hey," she said back. "Mr. Crane will be impressed that you're not late."

Jayson laughed, "Saw your pictures on your profile."

"You're not stalking me, are you?"

"Uh, no," Jayson stammered.

Goth Girl smiled and let out a small laugh, "Just busting your chops."

"Oh, yeah, funny," Jayson replied.

"So, what'd you think?" she asked.

"They are really good you know," Jayson said. "I even showed them to my sister, and she said the same thing."

"Why'd you do that?"

"Because they're good. And she's an artist too," Jayson explained. "Anyway, she thought they were good and she's going to apply to the Banff School of Arts."

"Really?"

"Well, I think so. She's still working it out," Jayson said.

"Cool."

"Yeah, it is."

She turned back to the book she was reading when Jayson first came into the class and then after a few seconds she turned around again.

"So, can you stop calling me Goth Girl then?" she asked.

Jayson blushed; he hadn't realized she knew. How'd she know?

He nodded, too embarrassed to speak.

Mr. Crane walked into the class and then after dropping his bag on his desk, he began to take attendance.

He got to the end of the list, where the W's were and called out, "Sadie."

Goth Girl smiled and answered, "Here."

CHAPTER 15

Wednesday was turning out to be one of Jayson's favorite days. His time at the soup kitchen never made him feel like an outsider, which most group activities always ended up doing.

In gym class, he was always sorted out into the non-athletic pile, kind of like the jock's version of the sorting hat in Harry Potter. Kids were not-so-randomly selected for teams and ensured the comfortable balance in the social pecking order amongst the students.

Jayson didn't mind. After all, when not much was expected of you, anything you did manage to do well was often met with astounding praise. Like Jayson's toilet basket during their first gym class. He didn't think it would have been as impressive if he had been on Moore's team as opposed to trying to outrun them.

"Anyone see Lucy?" Mr. Crane asked the three waiting in the parking lot.

Jayson, Moore and Goth Girl, sorry – Sadie, were waiting next to Mr. Crane's van, ready to leave for St. Agatha's soup kitchen, and all three shook their heads.

"I think she had a music class last today?" Jayson said. "I saw her in the hall when I was going into English class."

Mr. Crane looked at his watch, "We really should push off soon if we are going to get downtown in time to help set up today."

"I'll go check," Jayson offered and turned to run back into the school.

"You go as well, Sadie," Mr. Crane said. "In case you have to check the bathroom."

She nodded and then ran after Jayson, catching up to him when he was close to the door. The school was not as full as it was when they left for the parking lot fifteen minutes earlier, which made it easier to see down the length of the halls.

Jayson and Sadie looked through the windows of the doors to the classrooms as they ran down the halls. Jayson taking the right side, Sadie the left.

When they reached the end of the hall Jayson said, "Let's check the basement, maybe she is at her locker."

"You know where her locker is?" Sadie asked.

"No. You?" Jayson asked in response.

She shook her head, "Let's go before we are really late."

They took the steps two at a time and Jayson noticed how fast Goth Girl, sorry Sadie, really was. He wondered if she was ever on the track team.

Most of the lights were turned down in the cafeteria and all the chairs were lifted on top of the tables, ready for the cleaning staff to mop up the mess of food spills and footmarks.

"Lucy!" Sadie and Jayson both called out as they ran through the halls.

They would have completely missed her if Sadie hadn't noticed Lucy's bright purple bag leaning against the wall.

"Lucy! What're you doing down here?" Sadie asked. "Mr. Crane is wondering where you are."

She was sitting on the floor, her back pushed up against the wall. She had her legs pulled up close to her body and her face was pressed tight against her knees. Her sobbing was muted by her arms and legs, but her shoulders bounced with each cry.

"We should go get Mr. Crane," Jayson said.

"Screw that," Sadie said to him.

More of a warning than a statement and Jayson stood still. Sadie bent down on the ground and knelt beside

Lucy. She put her hand on Lucy's shoulder and began to speak in a low whisper.

"Hey, what's wrong Lucy?"

Lucy lifted her head slightly. Just enough to make eye contact with Sadie and then shook her head. She didn't speak.

"It's okay. You can tell me," Sadie reassured her. "You're shaking."

Lucy dropped her face back down and began to cry. This time loud enough that Jayson could hear her.

"Do you want me to have someone call your parents?" Sadie asked.

Lucy pulled her head up and wiped her tears with the back of her hand and then ran the back of her sleeve under her nose, "No, please, you can't call them."

Sadie shifted from kneeling to sitting, "Okay, then do you want to tell us what's wrong?"

"It's just everything," Lucy said pointing to her bag against the wall. "School, music, everything."

"I thought your marks were top of the class already?" Sadie said. "What's wrong?"

"They're good, but not high enough," Lucy said. Her tears and nose ran down her face and around the side of her mouth as she spoke. "You have no idea how much pressure I'm under."

"It's grade nine, Lucy," Jayson spoke for the first time. "How bad can it be?"

Sadie shot him a glare and Lucy dropped her face back down. Neither of them wanted his opinion. Fine with him. He was more comfortable being a sideliner anyway.

"Tell me how I can help you?" Sadie asked.

"You can't," Lucy said. "No one can."

Lucy looked at both Sadie and Jayson and shook her head.

"You don't know what it's like having the pressure I have at home. I need to not only have good grades; they need to be great. And they don't just need to be great, they need to be the top in the country. My parents moved to Canada so they could give their children the best life possible, and for them, that means the best school, the best job, the best opportunity. Do you know that I need to write the SAT at the same time students across North America are writing them for Harvard and Stanford - and it's already assumed that I'm going to get accepted?!"

"That's a lot," Sadie said.

"And, this weekend my parents are flying me to Toronto. Want to know why?" Lucy asked, now shaking and visibly furious.

Sadie nodded, "Why?"

"To audition for the top music camp for next summer. Prodigies, savants and freaks like me to learn how to be even better."

Lucy's breathing became more rapid and shallower. Jayson recognized the signs. He saw them enough.

"I think she's having a panic attack," Jayson whispered.

Sadie put her hand on Lucy's arm, "Is that's what's happening?"

Lucy nodded, "I usually can pull it together after I do some deep breathing, which is what I was trying to do when I was down here."

"We'll wait with you while you relax then," Sadie said. Reassuring Lucy the best she could.

Lucy took a deep breath, "I think if Mr. Crane comes down it'll be worse. Let's go. Maybe being at St. Agatha's will help distract me."

Jayson didn't know a lot about panic attacks, but he did know that ignoring them wasn't the way to deal with them. Riley proved that last January.

"If you're sure," Sadie said.

"I am," Lucy grabbed her bag and stood up straight. "Just please don't tell Mr. Crane. Or anyone else, please?"

"We won't," Sadie and Jayson promised in unison. Jayson knew all too well how hard it was having everyone know private things in your life that you would rather keep secret. And he couldn't tell if Sadie was just being nice or if she felt the same way that Jayson did, for the same reason.

Either way, the three walked back down the hall, through the cafeteria, up the stairs and out into the parking lot where Mr. Crane and Moore were waiting for them by the van.

Without saying a word to Lucy, Mr. Crane got into the van and unlocked the doors. The four climbed in. Moore and Jayson took the same two seats in the two rows in the back of the van, and Lucy and Sadie sat in the bench seat behind Mr. Crane. This time next to each other where Sadie could reassure Lucy that everything was going to be okay.

At least for today.

CHAPTER 16

A special meal was planned at St. Agatha's for the last Wednesday before the school's two-week winter break. Even though the soup kitchen itself didn't close, it would be the last time until after the new year that Jayson and the others would return.

Mr. Crane wouldn't reveal what exactly was planned but the giddy look he had on his face made Jayson wonder if it was going to be something he would regret. One thing he learned to expect from adults who got that look in their eye was that it always ended up being embarrassing.

The room at St. Agatha's which was normally set up for the soup kitchen's staff and patrons was now transformed into a tacky mall Santa's village.

Yep. Embarrassing.

Jayson could tell by the look of shock on everyone's face that they were thinking the same thing.

"Well, what do you think?" Mr. Crane asked, beaming a smile from ear to ear.

Jayson whispered to Moore who was standing next to him, "He can't think that the people who come here for sandwiches and soup are going to want this. Does he?"

Mr. Crane was oblivious to the kid's impression of the cardboard fireplace and paper stockings that were taped haphazardly to the far wall. He turned to look at the kids, "I know, great, huh?!"

The four nodded and smiled.

They knew the routine and what to do as they got ready for the meal rush which was due to arrive in less than half an hour. By the time the doors were opened, Jayson, Moore, Sadie and Lucy were positioned behind their tables, serving spoons in hand. And ready to pile the plates high.

Sadie spent the whole time talking to Lucy and giving her complete uninterrupted attention. Any time that Jayson tried to speak to her she just answered him quickly and then waved him away. Eventually, he gave up and tried to start a conversation with Moore.

One-word answers and gruff responses were all that Jayson was getting from Moore.

For the last few weeks, Moore had become even more of a jerk than Jayson thought he was. He was acting more like the kid who sucker punched him in the cafeteria and less like the guy with who he was laughing while watching the fail videos.

He was glad Moore never accepted his friend request after all.

He had given up expecting a conversation with Moore when he said, "You know, I should really be at practice instead of this stupid soup kitchen."

Jayson was about to make a comment and remind him that they were only there in the first place because of the fight he started in the cafeteria and that the only reason they only had to serve one day a week was because of Jayson's brilliant idea. Okay, well, it was more of a fluke that Mr. Crane put the idea of once a week at St. Agatha's instead of daily detention. But it was because Jayson pulled that flyer off the bulletin board in the first place. But instead, Jayson returned to mixing his spoon around in the mash potato tray in front of him.

"Ho! Ho! Ho!"

The sound echoed from the far end of the room.

Mr. Crane, poorly disguised as Santa Clause, entered through the main doors. The faded red velvet Santa suit was worn on the elbows and edges with many years of use. Rubbed and cleaned from years of kids spitting up (or throwing up) along with months between use where it was rolled up and stored away in a closet, gave the velvet a matted and dull look.

Mr. Crane patted his belly and walked around the tables, "Ho! Ho! Ho! Merry Christmas!"

Cheers and shouts came from the patrons who laughed and answered back with shouts of 'Merry Christmas'. The laughter of the patrons altered Jayson's initial impression that no one would want this.

Jayson couldn't help but smile at the ease at which joy and laughter began to fill the room. Even Moore managed to chuckle alongside the others as they watched Mr. Crane make his way around the room.

He pulled the heavy cloth sack that he had slung over his shoulder and dropped it on the floor by his feet.

"Who's been good this year?" he asked the crowd.

Arms shot up into the air and shouts of 'I have' came from everyone in the room.

Mr. Crane thrust his arm deep into the bag and began to pull out items and hand them to the crowd. Thick wool socks and mittens were passed around from one person to the next. Hats were given to those who needed them, and coats to those who had none.

Jayson watched, mesmerized, by the ease at which Mr. Crane filled a massive need with such a simple gift.

These people, Jayson thought, understood the value of this simple gift.

When Mr. Crane was finished, he disappeared into the back of the room to change out of his suit and get ready to take them home. Jayson carried his tray into the back with the others and began to wash them out.

When they were done, they waited near the door for Mr. Crane. The mood lightened in the room and spread over Moore, and Jayson could start to see his attitude lighten.

As Sadie and Lucy shared a joke, Moore turned to Jayson and smiled, "Did you see the latest fail video from GoonSquad45?"

And with that, the two boys connected.

CHAPTER 17

Sadie and Jayson agreed to try to spend some time with Lucy outside of their detention stint at St. Agatha's. Sadie's suggestion not Jayson's. And the most likely place to do that was during lunch. Jonnie had become part of their lunch crew somewhere along the line, and so far, had managed to keep his finger clear of his nose in front of the two girls.

They were sitting at a long table near the back corner and had a clear view of both doors. Jayson noticed Moore walking in with a group of guys. They were all dressed in matching maroon t-shirts and sporting matching backpacks with the basketball team logo embroidered on the side.

Jayson remembered seeing the pack the last time the group went to St. Agatha's.

Moore looked over and saw them and Jayson gave him a small wave. The kind of wave where you lift your hand a few inches off the table and toss in a small nod to try and look cool. Jayson couldn't master the looking cool part, but it could hardly be missed for anything other than what it was – a wave.

However, instead of a wave, a nod or even a smirk, Moore turned around and began to joke around with the guys he walked in with. Completely ignoring Jayson and the group.

Lucy was deep in the midst of explaining to Sadie the benefits of exploring the use of alternate colors in her wardrobe, and Sadie had been coming up with profile names for Lucy to use on the social media app that Sadie downloaded for her. Jonnie was listening to them, still in complete shock that he was this close to two girls, and that neither had asked him to leave.

"Red would look awesome on you with your dark hair," Lucy said.

"How about ViolinGirl as a profile name?" Sadie asked, ignoring Lucy's comment. "You know, because you play the violin."

"Duh," Jonnie said. Jayson rolled his eyes.

"My mom has some amazing material that she bought to make me a sari for my cousin's wedding. I should show it to you," Lucy said.

"How about Sharkarama?" Sadie asked with a laugh.

Lucy dropped her hands on the table, still holding her sandwich in her right hand, "Really? Sharkarama?"

"Just wanted to see if you were listening?" Sadie asked.

"Well, you're not taking this seriously."

"Okay," Sadie put down her phone and folded her hands together. "So, tell me, Miss Sharma, what should I be wearing?"

Lucy and Sadie had become close friends since the day they found her crouched in the corner of the basement. Lucy's anxiety attack left her vulnerable enough that she opened up to Sadie about her problems. About everything that was causing her stress in her life. And Sadie, as it turned out, was a good listener.

Afterward, at St. Agatha's, the two spoke nonstop through the meal service and found out they had more in common than either of them ever thought. And they bonded instantly.

Sadie's real name, as it turned out, was Sarah Williams and was born in London, England. She moved to Canada when she was partway through grade seven and spent the whole first year learning how not to speak with an accent.

Jayson thought it sounded really neat when Sadie proved to them that she, in fact, had a British accent and told her she shouldn't hide it. But Sadie said it just made her stick out and seem different and the other kids in her class teased her about it. That's when she decided it was better to fade away and fit in, instead of standing out and getting teased.

That, Jayson, could relate to.

With Sadie's help, Lucy was able to convince her parents to let her get a phone on the premise that it was where the top students and researchers were sharing ideas. Which wasn't altogether a lie.

To repay Sadie, Lucy insisted on helping her chose some colors to add to her wardrobe. Lucy said if you don't want to be called Goth Girl, then don't dress like one.

Now Jayson and Jonnie had spent the last week of lunches listening to them both volley profile name suggestions and clothing selections back and forth. But neither Jayson nor Jonnie had complained.

"Hey, how did you two get dragged into detention with Jayson?" Jonnie asked the girls. Jayson realized he never knew as well.

"One of Moore's stupid friends bumped into me and knocked me back into the table, so I gave him a push back," Sadie explained. "That's when Mr. Crane walked in."

"You?" Jayson asked Lucy.

"I literally was caught in the middle of two guys fighting and I guess it looked like I was involved," Lucy said.

Sadie rolled her eyes.

"Do you even know why they were fighting?" Jayson asked.

"Someone made a comment about Moore and a girl," Sadie said. "That's all I know."

"Has Moore talked to either of you outside of St. Agatha's?" Jayson asked.

Lucy and Sadie shook their heads.

"Why?" Sadie asked.

"I don't know. He just seemed like he was starting to be friendlier for a while and now he just seems angry," Jayson said.

"He's been friendly to me," Sadie said.

Jayson blushed at the idea that Sadie wanted Moore to be nice to her and thought that she was hoping for more. Lucy just shrugged her shoulders.

"Have you tried to speak to him?" Lucy asked, pointing out the obvious.

"No," Jayson said. "I mean, I see him in the hall sometimes because our lockers are close, and I say a quick hi."

"But nothing more?" Lucy asked.

Jayson shook his head.

"Maybe we should go to his basketball game tonight and support him. Just because he's popular doesn't mean he doesn't feel left out," Sadie said. "He always sees us together and maybe he feels weird coming over?"

"Or maybe he just thinks we're weird," Jonnie said, then took a large bite of his sandwich.

Sadie rolled her eyes and looked at Lucy and they both laughed.

Jayson smiled. And to think he was afraid of Sadie on the first day of school.

"Fine. The game starts at seven, do you want to meet there?" Jayson asked.

They looked at each other and then nodded. It was agreed. They were going to the game. Together. As friends.

"Noooooow," Lucy said (drawing out the tail end of the word) turning the conversation back to the more pressing matter, "Purple. Purple is the perfect color to start with. It's close to black, so it's not too far outside your comfort zone and it's popular this year so we can find lots of things for you to wear!"

Sadie thought about it and then nodded. Then her eyes shot up when she realized she thought of the perfect profile name for Lucy.

"Lulu!" Sadie shouted. "Your profile name can be 'LULU'."

They both laughed and then shook hands.

"Glad we got that settled," Jonnie said.

CHAPTER 18

The gym was packed with visitors from the opposing team's school as well as half the students from SOS. Jayson arrived at six-thirty and waited outside on the front steps for the others to arrive. Jonnie was first and then Lucy and Sadie arrived together, having been dropped off by Lucy's dad.

"Holy Crap!" Jayson said when he saw them walk up the front steps.

"Is she?" Jonnie asked.

"Yeah," Jayson said. "She's not wearing black!"

"Looks great, doesn't it?" Lucy asked.

Sadie blushed, still not used to the purple jeans and white sweater that Lucy picked out for her at the mall after school.

Jayson picked up on her discomfort and just smiled and gave him a thumbs up, "Let's go inside and see if we can get a spot to sit."

They ran up the front steps and down the hall to the gym. The bleachers were packed with a blend of students and parents who were present to cheer on the two basketball teams that were playing their final game before the two-week winter school break.

"There," Jayson pointed to the top row of the bleacher next to the door. "There's room up there."

The four weaved their way over bags and around bodies until they reached the top bench. They sat down and began to look around the gym. It was the first time that any of them had been to a school team function, opting for the privacy of their own homes on Friday evenings.

The squeaking sound of the player's shoes echoed in the cavernous gym as they practiced dribbling exercises and taking turns shooting at the net as they warmed up on the court.

Students cheered from either side of the gym shouting support for their team and heckling comments at the opposing team. Parents leaned in close to each other so they could hear their conversations over the noise.

The ref's whistle blew, and the crowd began to clap.

Jayson looked down at the SOS bench and spotted Moore who was the team captain. The team was in a circle facing Moore who was giving them a pep talk. Then suddenly they piled their hands atop of one another's and then with a shout they raised them in the air. They clapped as they broke away, five heading to the court and the rest to the bench.

The first two quarters saw the teams equally matched and they began the third quarter with a tied score of thirty-three.

Jayson noticed a group of kids at the far end of the bleachers pointing and looking down at the SOS team bench. It was the kid that was with Moore that Jayson thought he recognized.

Now that he could get a clearer view of his face, he realized he did recognize him, but he still couldn't pinpoint from where.

He was about to turn back to the game when he noticed the kid wave to Moore who just finished his shift and was now sitting on the team bench. Moore reluctantly smiled and nodded his head and then quickly turned his attention back to his team and began to cheer.

The game finally ended with SOS winning with a score of seventy-five to fifty-four. Students and parents began to stand and make their way down the steep bleachers as the teams were shaking hands.

"What do you want to do now?" Jayson asked.

Lucy and Sadie looked at each other and shrugged their shoulders.

"I have until ten-thirty before I have to be home," Lucy said.

"Me too," added Sadie.

"Let's get some pizza," Jonnie suggested.

"Great idea," Lucy said.

Jonnie blushed and the group began to walk down the bleachers following the crowd out the door.

Sadie grabbed Jayson's arm, "Why don't you ask Moore if he wants to come?"

"Are you serious?" Jayson asked.

"Don't look at me," Jonnie held his hands up. "I don't know the kid."

"And girls aren't allowed in the locker room, so it's up to you," Lucy said.

Jayson eyed Lucy and Sadie, "You both planned this didn't you?"

Neither answered, and Jayson knew it would be futile to argue with them.

"Fine, but I'm not promising anything."

Jayson agreed to meet them outside the school, and he started to walk against the flow of bodies and towards the school locker room. Jayson could never get used to the musty, stale smell of locker rooms and wondered why so many people who apparently cared about being healthy hung out in places that smelled so bad.

He plugged his nose and tried to breathe through his mouth.

He turned when he saw a group of guys from the basketball team walking towards him. He ran to the water fountain and started to drink, waiting for them to pass. When they had left, he started towards the locker room again. He contemplated turning around and just telling the girls that he couldn't find Moore, but he knew they would probably figure out that he was lying.

He heard a loud voice coming from around the corner; but not shouting.

"What's more important to you?" the angry voice was coming from an older man.

"You know that I am focused on that scholarship," snapped the younger voice, a kid Jayson's age.

"Then why are we even having this conversation?"

"It is just a small party," the kid begged.

"And we know what happened the last time I let you go to a party," the man snapped, but almost in a whisper.

"Please dad, I'll be the only one *not* there," the voice was Moore's.

"I don't care," the man snapped and then Jayson could hear his hand hit the metal locker. "You're not going if that kid is there."

"It doesn't matter!" Moore screamed. Jayson almost thought he heard his voice shake as if he was about to cry.

"It doesn't matter?" his dad asked in response. "It matters a whole hell of a lot if you want to get a scholarship to that college in the states."

Jayson stood with his back pressed against the wall, listening because he was too afraid to move and make a sound.

It was a few seconds before his father spoke again, "Look son, I can excuse the last time because I know you were drinking. No one needs to know. But if that happens again-."

"What?" Moore snapped. "You'll hit me like you did last time?"

Jayson risked being heard and took off down the hall. He turned the corner, running into a crowd of students walking towards the door and pushed his way through. Jayson stuffed himself in the crowd and pushed his way to the door, and then outside, where Sadie and the others were waiting.

They looked at Jayson when he emerged from the crowded steps.

"Did you find him?" Sadie asked, hopefully.

Jayson shook his head, "No, he must've left already."

"Good. Let's go," Jonnie said rubbing his stomach. "I'm starving."

CHAPTER 19

Jayson didn't know what to make of Moore's dad and realizing that the bruise on Moore's face a couple of weeks ago was courtesy of his own father. That was why Moore clammed up when Jayson asked him about it. And he had been evasive ever since.

Moore still hadn't accepted his follow request and Jayson had given up hoping he would. Maybe his sister was right and that it was all a statement of false friendships anyway. He just needed to focus on the friends he had now and the ones he was having fun with.

He pulled up Sadie's profile and saw some of the pictures she posted from the game and when they grabbed pizza after.

She still posted mostly abstract photographs and none of herself or their group, but they were really good. Like magazine good.

Some were in color, others black and white. But the ones that Jayson really liked were the ones where she played with the filters giving each picture a life of its own.

Jayson had six more followers, none of which he knew, and he felt odd being excited about them. He was focusing on the numbers, at least he could be honest about that. James had over one thousand followers and was posting photos of him and his new gang of friends.

They were playing hockey, going out for burgers and just generally having a great freaking time. While Jayson still mostly had a crappy social life.

He was scrolling through his feed when a notice flashed up on the top of his screen.

JayBart: You have one new follower.

He pressed the heart at the bottom of the screen and read the alert. LuLu is now following you.

Jayson smiled. LuLu. He could hardly believe that the profile name was even available.

She had posted some photos of her violin and even of her and her two younger sisters. But the one photo he stopped at was the one she posted last.

It was a selfie she took of the four of them as they were eating pizza. Jonnie, completely oblivious that he had sauce on his nose, and Jayson leaning in front of the three of them to make sure he fit in the photo.

All of them smiling.

CHAPTER 20

It was the first day of the two-week break from school and it was minus twenty-five outside. Frost covered the bottom of Jayson's bedroom window and he scraped away bits of ice with the tip of his finger.

He should be planning every day of the next two weeks and doing stupid best friend things with James. But instead, Jayson found himself feeling sorry for himself after receiving James' text saying he wasn't coming back for Christmas after all.

Jayson had convinced his dad to front him the money for two Jets tickets so he could surprise James with a night at the game. Now he was sitting with almost two hundred dollars' worth of tickets and no one to go with.

He was glad James had sent a text instead of calling because at least he could hide the fact he was super pissed off in a text.

Jayson's phone buzzed inside his pocket.

He ignored it. Probably just James making up some lame excuse as to why he backed out of coming home.

His phone buzzed again, and even though he tried, Jayson was unable to ignore it.

He pulled it out of his pocket and was about to toss it on his bed when he saw it was a text from Sadie. He unlocked his screen and read the whole text.

SADWILL:
heading to the mall to get my bro a gift
want 2 come?

Actually, Jayson thought, why not?

Half an hour later Jayson was stepping off the #64 bus and running towards the entrance to the mall. His face froze instantly the moment it hit the cold air. His jeans did little to protect his thighs from the burning feeling of the cold and he was pretty sure his toes were curling up inside his shoes.

He pulled his hat down as low as it would sit on his head and yanked up the collar of his shirt and held it over the tip of his frozen nose. Frost formed on his eyelashes where his breath rose across his face and he could feel the chill and the weight on his eyes.

He ran ahead of the frozen crowd from the bus and pulled the oversized glass door not waiting to hold it open for anyone behind him. He'll make it up to karma in the summer, he thought.

Sadie and Lucy were waiting on the bench near the food court where they agreed to meet.

"Oooh, you look cold," Sadie said as she did a mock shiver.

"And you don't," remarked Jayson.

"Lucy's dad gave us a ride," Sadie gloated.

"Yeah, this is one of those days where having an overbearing and protective parent ranks as a good thing," Lucy joked.

"Okay," Sadie said pulling both Jayson and Lucy back on track. "I need eight small gifts for my twerp of a brother."

"Why eight?" Jayson asked. "Especially if he's such a twerp."

"Our family celebrates Hanukkah, and it's the whole eight days of lights thing that my brother has spun into a guilt gift giving thing," Sadie said rolling her eyes.

Jayson imagined having to get eight gifts for both Shane and Riley, did some quick math, and shook his head.

"Oh, that could start to suck if you have a large family," Jayson said.

"Not really, it's a pretty cool holiday," Sadie said. "You both should come. Mom always lets us invite friends for one of the nights."

"I'll have to ask and make sure it's okay," Lucy said. "But my parents have met you so they'll probably be cool with it since it would be adding to my global knowledge."

"Did you call Jonnie?" Sadie asked.

"No, why would I?" Jayson asked.

"Because it would be a not-jerk thing to do," Sadie grabbed her bag and stood up. "Never mind. Let's get this over with. It's getting harder and harder to think of what to buy my brother."

"I'm guessing that's why I'm here," Jayson said.

"Well, yeah, but we're also friends numbnuts," Sadie punched Jayson in the arm.

Jayson laughed, holding back the wince from the sharp pain in his arm. He wondered if Sadie knew how strong she was.

"Does he like sports? You could get him a hat or something," Jayson suggested.

"Or a CD of a band he may like?" Lucy said.

"Hmm, he does like the Jets," Sadie said as they passed the sports store.

After buying a t-shirt from the sale bin (discounted because it had a slightly uneven hem), socks with the team's logo and a hat, they left the store.

"Great, now only five more gifts to go," Sadie said.

She had settled on random gifts from the kiosks in the mall and after an hour of searching had chosen a backpack with his name embroidered on the seam for the one large gift that she gave him every year.

"J-o-n-a-h," Sadie spelled out to the store clerk when she placed the order. "I can come back and pick it up in an hour if it'll be ready?"

The clerk said she would put it on a rush and gave Sadie a receipt to use when she picked it up.

"That was a pretty sweet bag you got your little brother," Jayson said.

"What are you getting your brother?" Sadie asked.

Jayson paused for a while and then without thinking he said, "I am going to take him to a Jets game over the Christmas holidays."

"Nice brother!" Lucy said. "It's a good thing I have sisters because I would have no idea what to get a brother."

Up until a minute ago, neither did Jayson. The brat better appreciate it.

"What about your sister?" Sadie asked.

Jayson thought about Riley and everything she had been through and couldn't think of an appropriate gift that he should get her.

"Crap," Jayson began to panic. "I don't have a clue!"

"Does she like clothes?" Sadie asked.

"Make-up?" Lucy asked.

Jayson shook his head to both of their questions.

"Music?"

"Books?"

"Movies?"

No. No. No.

"Wait," Jayson thought. "She's an amazing artist."

Sadie grabbed Jayson's shoulders and spun him around. They were standing in front of an artist's emporium store. Sadie and Lucy each grabbed one of Jayson's arms and pulled him inside.

They looked around for a selection of sketch paper, pencils and Lucy found a nice leather portfolio that Riley could use to store her drawings inside. Much better than her shelf, Jayson thought.

For the first time that he could ever remember he was excited about getting someone else a gift.

"Your sister is pretty lucky," Sadie said as Jayson was paying for the items.

The gift needed to be special. He couldn't bring himself to say it to his friends, but he almost lost Riley last January. The idea of not having her around to get this gift for started to make him feel nervous inside. He hadn't really thought about all the things he would miss having her around for.

Instead, he just said, "Yeah."

As they were leaving the store, Jayson stopped to look at the flyers that were taped to the artists' bulletin board near the exit.

“Hey, wait,” Jayson stopped in front of a flyer advertising a contest in the new year. “You should totally check this out, Sadie.”

Jayson pulled Sadie’s arm and pointed at the sheet that caught his eye.

“A contest?”

“Not just any contest,” Jayson corrected her. “You could win five thousand dollars!”

“It says ‘to the photographer who captures the essence of our city’,” Lucy read, flicking her hand in the air. “It’s being run by a lot of local businesses in the downtown area to promote our city.”

“It’s totally right up your alley!” Jayson said. “Five grand! Think about it.”

Sadie reached out and grabbed a flyer from the board and pulled it loose from the tack that was holding it in place. She folded it in half and shoved it into her pocket.

CHAPTER 21

"What do you bring to a Hanukkah dinner?" Jayson asked Riley.

"How am I supposed to know?" she said as she tried to straighten his shirt. "Now stand still if you want me to help you."

Sadie said 'sort of dressed up' which doesn't really help since he mostly still dressed in goth. Lucy was able to help her 'explore' different colors, but it was a slow transition that Sadie was taking her time with.

To Jayson's mom, 'sort of dressed up' meant a tie and shirt and clean pants. Jayson could get the clean pants part, and even the shirt, but the tie?!

"Look, if you get there and you think the tie is dork, then just take it off and stick it in your pocket," Riley suggested.

Jayson didn't think it was possible to look younger in a tie, but he managed to do just that. And the pimple that sprouted on the side of his cheek completed the prepubescent look. He started to rub it with his finger and Riley smacked his hand down.

"Don't or the cover-up will rub off," Jayson did not want to make a habit of his older sister putting make-up on his face.

"Loser," Shane yelled into Jayson's bedroom on his way down to the kitchen.

"He has no idea what I got him for Christmas this year," Jayson said. "That little twerp is going to regret that he said that."

Riley laughed, "I got him a sweatshirt. You definitely win this year."

Jayson watched his sister's reflection in the mirror as she tightened his tie, "Thanks Ry."

"No problem," Riley stood back to assess her work. "Not bad bro."

"At least I talked mom out of making me take flowers," Jayson said.

"Yeah, that would've been totally awkward," Riley agreed. "The chocolates are a better choice."

"Thank God for the internet."

"Yeah, God had a lot to do with that."

"Thanks for taking me to Sadie's place," Jayson said. "I know mom would have insisted on saying hello to her parents and everything."

"So, you and Sadie?" Riley asked. "Anything there?"

"Just friends Ry."

Riley put her hands up in that don't get defensive mode, "Just asking."

"Just saying," Jayson answered. "Can we go?"

Twenty minutes later Jayson was standing on Sadie's doorstep and ringing the doorbell. The ringing echoed on the opposite side of the door and was followed by the clicking of shoes on the tiled floor. The door swung open and Jayson was face to face with Sadie. Not the Goth Girl Sadie that he was used to, but the Sadie that Lucy had transformed.

"Hey, Lucy and Jonnie are already here," Sadie stepped back and held the door open so Jayson could walk inside.

He looked past Sadie at the guests in the living room and decided that the tie would remain in place.

"Here, this is for your mother," Jayson thrust the neatly wrapped box of chocolates towards Sadie.

She smiled and not wanting to make him feel awkward said, "My mom will like these a lot. Thanks."

After a quick introduction to both of Sadie's parents, they went to the basement where Lucy and Jonnie were hanging out with Sadie's cousins and friends.

"Your mom has a cool accent," Jayson said as they walked down the stairs.

"I'll be sure to let her know," Sadie said.

"No, please don't," Jayson pleaded before Sadie started laughing and he realized she was joking.

"Ha, very funny," he said. "I still think it would be cool if you didn't hide your accent."

"I'll take it under advisement," she joked.

They reached the bottom of the steps and Sadie began to introduce Jayson to the other kids their age in the room. And then she turned to the last person in the room.

"And this is my brother, Jonah."

"He's your brother?"

"He's your friend?"

And there at the bottom of Sadie's steps, in the midst of his first Hanukkah celebration, he was face to face with the crossing guard twerp that made it his job to torment Jayson every morning.

He took a deep breath and sighed.

It was going to be a long night.

***

Three days later Jayson returned the favor and invited Sadie, Lucy and Jonnie to his house for a Christmas celebration. Or his mother's version of a stuffed turkey that she was attempting with her experimental cooking.

"You are going to want to eat before you come over, however," Jayson warned his friends. "I'm not sure what my mom is going to pass off as turkey this year so I can't guarantee anything edible."

In contrast, at Sadie's Hanukkah dinner, Jayson indulged in a rich flavorful brisket and several cheesy potato latkes, with a healthy side of seconds. And when Sadie's mom came out with a cinnamon apple cake Jayson was sure he wept.

Today's meal was sure to illicit none of those reactions.

His friends arrived together, and Jayson was waiting for them by the front window.

"Hey guys," Jayson greeted them at the front door. The weather had not warmed above minus twenty-five and outdoor skating or tobogganing was put on hold.

"Hurry up," Jayson shouted as the cold air mass froze the front entrance.

Once everyone was inside and coats tossed in the backroom like at every good party, he quickly ran his friends through the crowd of family that was congregating in the living room. All trying to guess what Jayson's mom was going to surprise them with for dinner.

Jayson had warned his friends about the three P's so when he rushed through their introductions, none of them were surprised.

"And this is my Aunt Alice and Uncle Joe," Jayson kept his friends close to his side. "Sadie, Lucy, Jonnie." And he turned to leave.

"Is this your girlfriend?" Aunt Alice bellowed. Everyone stopped talking and turned to wait for Jayson's answer and the revelation that Jayson had managed what they thought was impossible.

Jayson's face reddened and he blushed ferociously. If he was able to speak, he would have stammered his way through an explanation but luckily, he didn't have to.

Riley, his favorite and most special sister, swooped in and saved the day.

"Aunt Alice, did I show you what Jayson got me for Christmas?" and Riley pulled his nosey aunt away from Jayson and his friends, giving them the chance to escape.

Dinner wasn't as bad as Jayson had thought it would be, in part because his mom had prepared 'real food' for the pleasure of the guests that were invited.

They ate off their laps in the television room and after they had finished the last of their strawberry dessert, Jayson turned on the television.

"Let's watch *The Sound of Music*!" Lucy pleaded.

"No way," Jayson argued. But secretly he also wanted to watch it and was going to let the girls win their argument.

Just as Captain Georg von Trapp was partway through singing Edelweiss, Aunt Alice stumbled through the room on her way back from the bathroom.

"I love this movie!" Aunt Alice cried. "I used to watch this all the time with my mother."

Jayson waited for his Aunt to leave the room, hoping against hope, that she wouldn't be reminded about her months' long harassment of him. He could feel her hot breath as she stood behind the couch watching the movie.

The sweet smell of wine drifted down over Jayson, until suddenly a flood of tears came, "Jayson why won't you just tell me what your nana said to you?"

"Oh, crap!" Jayson mumbled and threw his hands over his face.

He just kept repeating 'please go away' in his head, but she just kept weeping from where she was standing.

"It's all I have left of her, Jayson! Why are you being so selfish! I know there was something she wanted to say, and she would have said it to me if you weren't there. Always hovering about like you were!"

Jayson could feel the combination of Aunt Alice's hot breath and random drops of spittle that always accompanied her speech after three glasses of wine.

"Aunt Alice, please," Jayson begged. "My friends are here!"

"I always said your mom pampered you too much! She pampered all her kids too much! That's why Riley -."

Jayson didn't let her get any further into her sentence and he jumped off the couch and turned to face her.

"You are a miserable old drunk, you know! Your kids are a miserable nuisance and the only reason we even go over to your place is that my mom feels sorry for you because Uncle Joe is always off on his hunting trips," Jayson could feel the heat rise in his face. "And don't ever mention anything negative about Ry. EVER!"

Jayson was shaking and he could feel the tension in his arms as his hands clenched into fists. Balled together and ready to fly.

Aunt Alice began to shake and stared at Jayson in shock. His Uncle Joe came running to pull Aunt Alice away from him before anything else was said, while the three P's stood completely oblivious to what was going on around them.

Jayson's mother was standing by Riley with her arms wrapped around his sister's shoulders. And on Riley's face wasn't a look of embarrassment or shock but of relief.

Riley mouthed the words 'thank you' and Jayson could feel the tension release from his body and his breathing slowed.

A hand rested upon his shoulder and he turned around and Sadie was standing behind him. Smiling.

And for the first time since James left, he had a friend who he knew had his back.

CHAPTER 22

With family dysfunctions out in the open, their friendship was off to a more comfortable start in January. Jonnie, as it turned out, didn't know who his father was, and he revealed this on the night of Jayson's outburst against his Aunt Alice as a way of trying to make him feel better.

How did Jayson not ever know that? He knew Jonnie for years.

Jayson was starting to realize that Jonnie was more resilient and forgiving than he ever would have given him credit for. He just wished Jonnie could just stop picking and flicking.

Their first day back at school was also the first Wednesday of the year, which meant a stint at St. Agatha's.

Jayson had almost forgotten the stale and cold smell of the church basement when they would first arrive. The hours of it sitting vacant during the day along with the poor insulation meant it took a couple of hours to warm up and absorb the scent of the meal being cooked for the patrons.

The city had seen an extreme dip in temperatures over the last few weeks and Mr. Crane told them to expect a few extra people arriving for warmth and food at St. Agatha's.

When Moore climbed into the van, Jayson was suddenly reminded of the last time he saw him. He was standing by his locker arguing with his father after the basketball game.

Jayson never told Sadie, Lucy or Jonnie what he had heard, and he thought that no matter what a jerk Moore could be, that he deserved some privacy. Plus, he was super uncomfortable with the fact he knew his father slugged him.

Moore wasn't talkative and he didn't push a conversation as they stood in their same spots serving scoops of mashed potatoes and beans to hungry visitors.

They had been there an hour when Jayson asked, "Hey, did anyone see Pesky Pete?"

Pesky Pete was a nickname that Pete, a regular to St. Agatha's, gave himself. He was always quick with a joke and to ask for seconds, thirds and fourths. And the one sure smile that Jayson and the others were sure to get while working at St. Agatha's.

They had all shook their heads. No one had seen him.

When they were finished serving, the last of the visitors had left and they began to clean up, Mrs. Crane pulled them aside.

"Sit down for a minute, kids," Mrs. Crane said, and she pulled some chairs together.

Everyone sat down and Jayson got a bad feeling in the pit of his stomach. The kind of feeling you get when you know you cheated on a test question and you were going to be called out for it in front of the class. But this wasn't a test or their class.

"I have some sad news to tell you," Mrs. Crane took a deep breath. "Mr. Fitch has passed away."

They looked at Mrs. Crane perplexed. It was sad that Mr. Fitch died, but none of them knew who he was.

"I'm sorry, you kids knew him as Pesky Pete."

The air was suddenly sucked from Jayson's lungs. His nana was the only other person he knew who had died, but she was old. Pesky Pete was about his father's age.

"How?" Jayson blurted out, and he could feel tears come to his eyes and he didn't care to wipe them away. He didn't care that anyone saw him cry either.

"He was sleeping outside, like many of our visitors who come here in the evening do, because they have nowhere else to go," Mrs. Crane explained.

"But I thought that they used the shelter on Main Street at night?" Jayson asked.

"Some do," Mrs. Crane said. "But they don't have enough beds for everyone. They, like most organizations who are helping the homeless, are short funded. We barely make monthly payments and if it wasn't for volunteers like you kids, and the men and women who come to cook in the day, we couldn't get these meals out."

Jayson felt like he had been punched in the gut. The pain he was feeling was a real physical pain and he suddenly was flooded with guilt for being angry at his mom for not having 'real food' around the house.

"I'll give you kids some time," Mrs. Crane stood. "Don't worry about cleaning up today."

Jayson looked over at Lucy and she had her face buried in her hands and she was sobbing. Sadie had her arm wrapped around Lucy's shoulders and she was trying to comfort her while she wiped away her own tears.

Moore had dropped his elbows to his knees and hung his head down. Jayson couldn't see his face, but he knew how he was feeling.

They sat there for half an hour until Mr. Crane arrived to take them home. They rode the entire distance home in silence and when they reached Jayson's house, he jumped out of the van and waved a silent goodbye and walked into his house.

He walked upstairs, into his room and closed the door. He lay flat on his bed and stared at the ceiling wondering why someone like Pesky Pete deserved to die.

Why anyone deserved to die. And who chooses? He was going to ask Father Monahan that on Sunday. He had been wanting to ask him that ever since Riley tried to kill herself and his grandmother died.

Jayson wasn't sure how long he was laying on his bed when his phone began to buzz.

Instinctively he reached out and grabbed his phone.

It was a group chat that Sadie sent out.

SADIE:
i know what we can do

JAYSON:
4 what?

SADIE:
to remember Pesky Pete

JAYSON:
what is it?

LUCY:
?

JONNIE:
who's Pesky Pete?

JAYSON:
a guy from St. Agatha's who died

JONNIE:
oh...
bummer

JAYSON:
what r u going to do?

SADIE:
raise 5G for the shelter for more beds

JAYSON:
how?

SADIE:
the picture contest. . .
the one you made me think about
i'm doing it

JAYSON:
cool

LUCY:
nice

JONNIE:
what contest?

JAYSON:
you can win 5 grand with pictures of the city

JONNIE:
i don't have pictures of the city
but I'll try. . .

JAYSON:
not u numbnuts – Sadie!

JONNIE:
makes sense
she's good

SADIE:
i need your help tho
to get more shots around town
i'm going to need a lot

LUCY:
count me in

JONNIE:
me 2

JAYSON:
me 3

MOORE:
count me in too

CHAPTER 23

"I don't see why there's any reason that I have to go to church!" Jayson gave a muffled scream from under his covers.

His mom was standing over him dressed and ready to leave. Jayson had hoped that if he pretended to be asleep and waited out his mom under his covers that he may have a chance to win the battle and stay home.

He was wrong.

Not only did his mom work out every inevitable delay that may occur, she also was prepared for the onslaught of excuses that were sure to come her way.

"Actually, I'm surprised that you haven't tried this sooner," she said.

Jayson flung the comforter cover off his face and slammed his arms by his side and looked up at his mom.

"Just give me one good reason why I need to go?" Jayson asked.

"I'll give you two. Riley and Shane, they both would like you there," his mom crossed her arms over her thick yellow sweater and stared down at Jayson. "And your nana, so that's three. Your nana always thought that we should go to church more as a family so there's that."

"But I have a lot of homework to do," Jayson said.

"You told me yesterday that you were all caught up."

"Crap," Jayson said.

"Yeah, that's your inside voice I think," his mom said. "And one you're probably going to want to leave home and not bring to church."

"I am not going!" Jayson declared. "It doesn't make a difference anyway."

His mom unfolded her arms and placed her hands on her hips, "Well, I will say I'm disappointed."

And there it was. The disappointment splayed across Jayson's mom's face. Along with the guilt was the sharp pang of a knife being plunged deep inside of him. He didn't know how, but his mom could always win any argument with the 'I'm disappointed' card.

Why didn't she just start with that one?

Jayson folded the comforter back and swung his legs over the side of the mattress.

"I'll be down in five," Jayson said, in his best defeatist voice in one last ditched attempt at sympathy.

His mom waved the tips of her fingers at him over her shoulder as she walked out of his room, "Don't forget to brush your teeth."

Twenty minutes later they were rushing into Sacred Heart Catholic Church and after a quick splash of holy water and a hurried sign of the cross, they slid into the row at the back of the church just as Father Monahan was beginning his weekly service. Jayson ran his tongue over the front of his teeth and cringed at the film and dryness in his mouth. He heard a hollow growl, and he tightened his stomach muscles and grabbed the front of his shirt with his hands, in a failed effort to erase his hunger.

It didn't help and once the mass was over and the congregation departed for the coffee and donuts in the basement Jayson used the opportunity to break away from the crowd.

He reached out and grabbed his dad's elbow, "I see a friend from school. I'm just going to say hi and I'll meet you by the car."

His dad nodded and turned to follow the crowd down the hall.

Jayson then called out to his dad, "Oh, can you get me a donut?"

His dad smiled and gave him a thumbs up. If they weren't standing in the church and hadn't come to realize the true value a sugar laden treat garnered in their house, it would have been an embarrassing move.

Jayson waited until his dad disappeared into the crowd and then through the doors that led to the basement, until he turned to walk out the doors of the church.

"Jayson, are you not going to join everyone for a treat?" Father Monahan asked. "You know, I think sometimes it's the only reason most of the congregation comes."

Father Monahan laughed at his too-often-told joke and Jayson nodded awkwardly.

"How's everything going Jayson?" Father Monahan asked.

"With Riley? Better."

"That's good. But I meant with you."

"Oh, well, fine. I guess."

"You guess?" Father Monahan asked. "You're not sure?"

"It's just that the year has been a lot tougher than I thought it was going to be in September," Jayson said.

"Grade nine has a way of doing that. How is your volunteer work going at St. Agatha's?"

Jayson shrugged his shoulders, "It's alright. Kind of sad last week and all."

"Ah, yes, Pesky Pete passed away," Father Monahan nodded his head. "It was very sad news to get."

"Father," Jayson asked. "Why is it that some really crappy things happen to good people? How do you keep going and keep telling people that everything is going to be alright?" Tears began to come and no matter how hard Jayson tried to hold them in they came with a rush and he couldn't stop them.

Father Monahan steered Jayson away from the door and over to an empty pew at the back of the church. When they were seated, he handed Jayson a tissue. Jayson wiped his eyes. His emotions came all flooding out.

"I imagine it's affected you even more because we're coming up on a year since your sister Riley tried to commit suicide," Father Monahan said.

There! Father Monahan could say the words, why couldn't his mother?

"It just doesn't make any sense if you say God cares about people who are good, then why doesn't he protect them? Why do good people have to suffer?" Jayson asked.

"Jayson, I can quote you a verse from the Gospel of Peter, but I don't think that's what you're looking for. What I can say is that what God gives us is a chance to join together and help each other. God can't protect you from getting hurt if you fall off your bike, only you can do that by being careful and wearing a helmet. He can't stop wars, illnesses or violence but he gives us tools and compassion from his lessons to learn how to deal with these tragedies and then hopefully we can move forward and grow."

Jayson looked up at the empty church and the statues staring down at him, "It's just so hard to understand."

"I agree," Father Monahan said.

"You do? I thought that since you're a priest that you don't question why bad things happen to good people?"

Father Monahan's bellowing laugh echoed in the empty church, "Jayson, that is the exact reason why I believe what I do is so important. We all have doubts sometimes, even he did."

Father Monahan pointed at the statue of Jesus in the vestibule at the side of the church.

"It's hard to believe sometimes," Jayson said pointing to the same statue. "You know, in him."

"I know. And that's okay. You can have as many questions as you want about God just remember to search out the answers in your heart and remember, even if you find doubt, you'll always be welcomed back."

Jayson wasn't sure how long he spoke with Father Monahan in the back pew of the empty and cavernous Sacred Heart Church; but when they were finished he had told Father Monahan about his doubt with his friendship with James, his lack of friends, his uncertainty with his new friends, his fear in losing Riley and the secret that his nana burdened him with on her death bed.

When he left the church, he wasn't closer to resolving his doubt in God, but he was closer to believing that by focusing on a positive message, that he was at least heading in the right direction.

CHAPTER 24

The contest closed on January tenth and they had three days to assemble some of Sadie's amazing photos and submit them in the contest.

"The application also says the photos need to be accompanied by a three-page essay as to why the city is so special to me," Sadie said. "I don't think I can get everything done in time!"

"Leave the essay to me!" Lucy promised. "I will write a kickass essay that they can't ignore!"

"Language, Lucy!" Jayson scolded.

She smiled, "I can work on that while you help Sadie get some photos together."

Moore, for the first time in months, seemed to have been re-energized and actually pleasant to be around. He didn't even seem to mind Jonnie hanging around them.

They agreed to meet early Saturday morning at the mall where Sadie had a plan mapped out. She was going to take them on a tour of the city through the eyes of those who are homeless.

"Let's show the downtown business group a side to the city that none of them see," Sadie said. "One that they are fortunate enough to not need to see."

"But won't that be a little depressing if you want to win the contest?" Jayson asked.

"Good point," Jonnie added.

"We can show the need of this side of the city but still show the beauty in the people," Sadie said.

Jayson was sure he could hear a slight inflection of a British accent in her voice.

He didn't mention it.

Sadie had mapped out each bus route in the city and with intermittent stops for hot chocolates and burgers, they covered the areas of the city that she had planned on by seven-thirty.

"It's dark. We should probably get home," Jayson said.

"You want a ride?" Moore asked the group.

"Uh, sure," Jayson answered for them.

Moore called his mom and fifteen minutes later she pulled up in front of the coffee shop where they were waiting. They piled into Moore's SUV and one by one his mom drove them home.

Jayson's house was the last one on the route and he was dropped off last.

“It’s the blue house on the right, Mrs. Moore,” Jayson leaned forward looking out the front window.

The SUV pulled up in front of his house and he opened the door, “Thanks for the ride Mrs. Moore. Bye.”

“You’re very welcome. It’s nice to finally meet some of Matt’s friends.”

Jayson closed the door and waved as they drove away.

He ran inside and took a long hot shower and only turned it off when the water began to dribble cool.

He changed into his pajamas and crawled into bed. Tonight, was not a night he wanted to stay up late.

Jayson closed his eyes and his body felt as if it was floating, the way it does when you begin to drift asleep when his phone buzzed on his night table. The sound echoed through his room and he reached over and grabbed his phone.

He flipped it over and read the alert on the screen.

JayBart: You have one new follower.

Jayson slid the lock on the screen to see his new follower’s name. MattMoore.

CHAPTER 25

Lucy's recital was being held at the Concert Hall and they all agreed they would go to support her. Even Moore agreed he would come along, and Jonnie, to Jayson's surprise, had continued to avoid doing anything too embarrassing.

The deep freeze that set in over the last month was starting to ease but Jayson wasn't sure as he stood shivering under the lighted overhang at the Concert Hall waiting for his friends to arrive.

Moore arrived first. His mom dropped him off at the corner of the street and he ran the remainder of the way to the front steps. He took the steps two at a time and landed with a thud next to Jayson.

"It's freezing out here," he slapped Jayson on the arm. "Let's go inside. We're going to freeze our balls off."

Jayson laughed and followed Moore inside to the front lobby where they waited for Jonnie and Sadie to arrive.

Jayson looked up at the ceiling which extended the full height of the seating area inside the concert hall area. Tiered levels and walkways were filled with people sharing a drink before the performance and meandering through the collection of local paintings that were being displayed in the upper lobby.

The Junior Arts and Music Association, also known as JAMA, had combined their efforts to promote the orchestra and the visual artists in the city and was putting on a huge fundraiser in the Concert Hall which was normally reserved for performers like Il Divo, which Jayson's mom dragged his dad to; or Rick Mercer, which Jayson's dad dragged his mom to; or Mini Pops, which Shane dragged his parents to.

"I've never been here before," Jayson said as he stretched his neck and twisted around to get a full view of the inside of the building. "Have you?"

"Once," Moore said. "But that was when I was a kid. My mom dragged me to The Nutcracker."

Jayson arched his eyebrows and looked at Moore. The two boys broke out into a hysterical laugh at the word Nutcracker. An elderly couple shot them a disapproving look and they quickly suppressed their laughs.

"Let's get a coke," Moore suggested and before Jayson could answer he began to walk towards the concession stand.

They took their place in the line up behind three couples waiting to place their order.

"I had no idea that Lucy was this good!" Jayson said.

"Well, we haven't heard them yet. But they must be pretty good to be here," Moore agreed.

"Didn't your team play at the MTS Centre in October?" Jayson asked.

Moore nodded, "Yeah. Did you come?"

"Nah," Jayson said. "I had some other plans. But that must've been cool."

"It was. My dad was pretty hyped because there were going to be some scouts from Universities there," Moore and Jayson took a step forward as the line moved. "He spent more time working the crowd than watching me."

Jayson nodded as Moore spoke and he noticed that Moore's smile turned into a frown at the mention of his dad.

"Hey, the game before the Christmas break was awesome," Jayson said, changing the focus of the conversation away from Moore's dad.

Moore's eyes brightened, "You came?"

"Yeah, we all did," Jayson said. "Sadie, Lucy, Jonnie. We went for pizza after."

Moore nodded.

"We looked for you," Jayson quickly added. "But we couldn't find you after."

The line moved and they stepped into the second spot.

"We have a big game next week, you should come," Moore said.

Jayson smiled and nodded. He could hardly believe Moore was inviting them, the losers of the group, to his game.

"Hey, what's up with Mr. Samson's science project?" Moore asked. "Is he serious about us needing to grow mold in a dish? That's so disgusting."

"No shit," Jayson said.

"Young man!" the woman in front of them turned around and shot Jayson a stern look. "Language!"

Moore jabbed Jayson in the ribs and quietly laughed. It was totally worth the embarrassment, Jayson thought.

"Hey, I thought we were meeting out front?" Sadie wacked Jayson on the back.

She and Jonnie were still shivering and wearing their coats pulled closed.

"Sorry, it was too cold out," Jayson apologized.

"No kidding," Jonnie said, his teeth chattering.

The announcement came on the loudspeaker alerting them that the concert was going to start in ten minutes.

They left their spot in line just as the people in front of them grabbed their order. They headed to the door on the far left that led to where their seats were in the mezzanine section of the concert hall.

The concert lasted an hour and a half with one intermission, during which they were also unsuccessful at getting a drink, and it was decided that they would wait for Lucy and grab a pizza together after the show.

Until ten-thirty the five teens joked, laughed and ate pizza. When it was time to leave, Sadie's dad was waiting out front to drive them all home.

"That's okay, I have my own ride," Moore said, and he waited behind as the others climbed into the car.

Jayson climbed into the back seat and was pushed up against the window of the car. As they were pulling away from the Pizza Palace Jayson saw Moore inside, where he high fived the same guy that he saw him with after school months ago and was also at the basketball game.

Now Jayson was sure he knew him. But what was Moore doing with him?

CHAPTER 26

The winner of the photo contest was being revealed Saturday afternoon and that morning they agreed to wait at Sadie's with her for the announcement. Lucy's mom made a dessert treat that she brought with her when she arrived.

"It's called Gulab Jamun," Lucy said. "They're like a donut ball but with sticky syrup on them."

This, Jayson knew, his mom would not add to their experimental menu and he quickly grabbed one of the sweet-smelling doughy treats.

He popped one into his mouth and he could feel the sugar sink into his tongue. He recalled the dessert his mom offered up the night before and it was all he and his brother and sister could do to not choke on it. It was his mom's version of apple cake. But without the sugar, flour or butter. Basically, it was a powder puck with dried chopped apples.

Then a frightful thought occurred to Jayson, what if his mom's experimental cooking phase wasn't a phase, and it was her new way of cooking!

Jayson reached over and took another ball before he was finished with the first one.

"When are they announcing the winner?" Lucy plopped down on the couch and curled her legs under her body.

"Sometime this afternoon," Sadie said.

Jayson noticed Sadie was nervously rubbing her hands together and red marks were showing along her knuckles and palms.

"Hey," Jayson said nodding to Sadie's hands. "You're going to win. Don't worry."

Sadie separated her hands and slipped them under her legs. "You don't know that."

Jonnie took a bite from the sweet sticky ball in his hand and agreed with Jayson, "You're totally going to win the five grand." Then Jonnie raised his hands as if he was a grandstand preacher. "I can feel it!"

The four of them laughed and Lucy tossed a pillow in Jonnie's direction.

Sadie's phone began to buzz from where she left it perched on the table.

They all stopped laughing and looked at the phone that continued to buzz.

"Answer it!" Jayson yelled.

Lucy leaned forward on her legs, "Answer it!"

Sadie reached forward and picked up her phone. She slid the green bar to the right, "Hello?"

"Speaking," Sadie said.

They watched as Sadie nodded her head as the other person on the phone was speaking and she listened to what they had to say without responding except for the occasional 'Uh-huh' or 'Okay'.

She dropped her chin down and covered her face with her right hand and then thanked the person on the phone before hanging up. Sadie's shoulders bounced and they could hear her muted sobs behind the pressure of her hand over her mouth.

"I'm sorry Sadie," Jayson said. "I totally thought you had it in the bag."

Sadie lifted her face to the group and what Jayson and the others thought were sobs of sadness, were actually tears of joy. She jumped up from her seat and with a huge smile, she shouted, "I won! My photos won!"

They all jumped up from where they were sitting and started to congratulate each other, even though it was Sadie's photos that were entered in the contest.

Sadie grabbed Lucy's hands, "They said my photos were incredible, but it was the essay that clinched the decision between me and the runner up!"

The two girls jumped up and down, turning in circles shouting.

Sadie's parents ran into the room when they heard the shouts from the other end of the house. Sadie turned when she heard them come it.

"I won!" Sadie ran over to her parents and dove into their open arms and they too jumped up and down and in circles.

"We need to tell Moore!" Jayson said, thinking about the fifth person who helped them tackle the photos around the city on that ultra-freezing Saturday.

"Call, don't text," Sadie said. "I want to hear his voice."

Jayson dropped his eyes to Sadie as if to say 'really?'

"What?" Sadie blushed, "I just want to hear him freak out. He's always so calm and cool about everything. It's not normal."

Jayson pulled up Moore's contact and pressed call. He couldn't remember the last time he made an actual call from his phone. Outside of calling one of his parents to pick him up from somewhere. But parents don't count when it comes to phones.

"It's ringing," Jayson said, as if it were some sort of great revelation.

The phone answered on the third ring, "Hello." But it wasn't Moore's voice. It was the voice of a woman.

"Uh, sorry," Jayson said. "I was trying to call a friend."

"Are you trying to call Matthew?" the woman said.

Jayson was about to say no, but then realized that was Moore's actual name, "Yeah I was."

The woman's sobs morphed into her next sentence, "Are you the young boy I dropped off after the day he was out taking pictures downtown?" she asked.

"Yeah, my name is Jayson," he answered.

"Matthew is in the hospital, Jayson. He's – he's, oh, he's had an accident," she cried.

"Is he okay? What happened?" Jayson asked, the others now sensing that something was wrong.

"I'm not sure. Look I have to go now but call back tomorrow and I will let you know more."

Moore's mom ended the call without saying goodbye.

Jayson got a bad feeling after speaking with Moore's mom. She had the same sound in her voice that his mom had after Riley was rushed to the hospital when she spoke to her friends.

He looked up and said, "We need to go to the hospital. Now."

CHAPTER 27

The contest and the five grand all seemed unimportant as they drove to the hospital. Sadie's dad grabbed his keys and rushed out to the driveway. They followed him out and sat in silence the entire way to the hospital. Each of them, Jayson was sure, trying to figure out what happened.

They arrived at the front entrance and piled out of the car. Sadie told her dad that she would call when they needed a ride home as she ran into the hospital behind Jayson.

They frantically rambled off their explanation to the guard at the front desk that they were there to see a friend and after they gave them Moore's full name, the guard directed them to the floor where he was being treated.

In the elevator, they rode the nine floors in silence along with three other visitors who were carrying a potted plant. The elevator bell rang as they reached their floor and the doors slid open.

They fell out of the elevator, Jonnie almost tripping on his left shoelace, and followed the sign to the nurse's station.

"We are here to see Matthew Moore," Jayson said.

The nurse ran her finger down the list and looked up," I'm sorry. Only family is allowed in."

"But we're his friends," Jayson said, realizing how odd that sounded and wondering if Moore felt the same way.

"Jayson?" the woman standing behind Jayson asked.

He spun around and came face to face with Moore's mom who was returning from the cafeteria with two cups of coffee. Her hair was pulled back in a ponytail and her pale face exaggerated her red rimmed eyes from hours of crying.

Jayson stared at Moore's mom, frozen in place, remembering the night that Riley was taken to the hospital and how no one knew what to say to him when he asked.

"Is he okay?" Jayson finally asked.

Moore's mom looked behind her into the waiting lounge, "Why don't you come with me in here." She turned around and walked into the empty room and Jayson and the others followed her.

When the door was closed and they were all sitting down, Moore's mom spoke. "What I'm going to say is hard. But I think it's worse to hide it from people who care about Matthew. He's going to need all the friends he can get."

Jayson waited for her to continue, not wanting to interrupt her.

And as she began to speak Jayson slipped back to last January when Riley was rushed to the hospital after swallowing a bottle full of pills. The words were the same, but the name of the patient was different. Words like 'depressed', or 'We didn't know he was feeling like this' or 'Did you see anything?' All were part of Moore's mom's explanation, hoping to get a glimpse into why he would have tried to hurt himself.

"When he's ready I will call you. Right now, we just need to let the doctors take care of him," Moore's mom explained.

She thanked them for coming and then walked out of the lounge and headed back to Moore's room. Jayson ran out after her.

"Mrs. Moore," Jayson said as he came up behind her. "My sister, Riley. She also tried, well she, last January." Jayson tried to get the words out but instead, a flood of tears came. Moore's mom grabbed Jayson and pulled him close. They both stood in the hall gripping onto each other. Strangers, really. Crying. No words needed to be exchanged and she understood that Jayson knew exactly what she was feeling.

She straightened her arms and looked into his eyes, "It'll be okay. Matthew has a lot of friends who care about him. We will get him the help he needs and work together. Okay?"

Jayson nodded and wiped the tears from his face with the back of his hand.

"It's like I told Christopher who came by earlier, we can do this together," Moore's mom said.

Jayson nodded, and then it clicked. "Christopher Gibson?"

"Yes, I imagine you all know each other. Look I have to get back to Matthew."

The puzzle that was Moore suddenly clicked into place. Jayson returned to where his friends were waiting, and they called Sadie's dad and headed home.

CHAPTER 28

A week after Moore was released from the hospital, his mom phoned Jayson and asked her to come by and visit him. Jayson didn't tell Sadie, Lucy or Jonnie because he thought it would be better to come by on his own. He had his mom take him to the bookstore before he came so he could get a selection of sports magazines and some cookies. That, along with the write up in the paper about Sadie's photo contest win was stuffed in a green plastic bag that he carried in his left hand.

Even though it was cold out, Jayson was shivering for another reason. He was nervous. Seeing his sister after she came home from the hospital was different. And even though he told Moore's mom that they were friends, he had only known Moore since the beginning of grade nine, and only because they were in detention together.

"Jayson, I am so glad you are here," Moore's mom took his thick winter coat and hung it in the front closet.

"You can go on up, his room is on the left at the top of the stairs."

Jayson walked up the stairs and past the family photos lined on the wall. He noticed most of them were sports related and an older photo of his father was of him in his university jersey caused Jayson to stop and look. "What the-?!"

Jayson walked up the stairs and just as he was wondering which room was Moore's he noticed his name on the door in hand-painted letters, like the one's his mom had on his door up until he was twelve. He knocked on the door.

"Come in," Moore said.

Jayson turned the handle and stepped into the room. Moore was sitting on a chair, tilted back on the two rear legs, and was playing a video game on his screen. The room was not unlike his. That is if you don't count the line of sports trophies and jerseys on his wall.

"Hey," Jayson said.

"Hey," Moore said. "Wanna play?"

"Sure," Jayson dropped the bag to the floor and grabbed the controller that Moore held in his outstretched hand.

For the next hour, they played numerous rounds of Firepower Elite with the extent of their conversation ranging from 'oh no!' and 'watch out' to 'loser' when one of their avatars was finally shot down.

Moore's mom knocked on the door and walked in with a tray of cookies and two cans of pop.

Jayson pulled the tab and took a long swig, this too, was an illegal substance in Jayson's house.

They sat awkwardly for a few minutes drinking their pop and nibbling on cookies when Jayson thought Moore was about to ask him to leave.

"Hey, my mom said you came to the hospital that night," Moore said.

"Yeah," Jayson answered.

"Thanks."

Jayson nodded as if to say, 'no problem'.

Then he blurted out, "My sister, Riley, swallowed a bottle of pills last January. It totally freaked us all out."

There it was, not planned and not tactful, but out. Jayson needed to work on that.

Matt looked down at the can in his hand and nodded, "Yeah, it was a pretty shitty thing I did to my parents."

"To your whole family. Everyone thinks it just affects the parents, but it totally threw my brother and me for a while."

"Why did your sister do it?" Moore asked.

"She was suffering from anxiety. For a bunch of reasons, and she just didn't see a way out back then," Jayson explained.

"And now? How is she?" Moore asked.

"Good. Better. She said she will always need to deal with it, but she goes to a therapist and she seems to be herself again," Jayson explained.

"My mom has me going to a therapist too," Moore said. "The guy is kinda nice, I guess."

The silence returned between them and before Jayson had a chance to stop himself, he said, "I remember where I thought I knew your friend from."

"Who?" Matt asked.

"Christopher Gibson."

Matt, to Jayson's surprise, wasn't shocked or mad, "You know him?"

"Yeah, we were in school together, but he left after grade seven," Jayson said.

"How well do you know him?" Moore asked.

"Pretty good," Jayson said.

"Then you know?" Moore asked, not making eye contact with Jayson.

"That he's gay? Yeah."

"And you don't care?"

"No, why would I. He's still a goofball," Jayson said.

Moore laughed, "Yeah, I know."

"Does he still make that stupid tapping noise with his foot?"

"Totally, it drives me nuts."

"Mrs. Wardell, our grade seven teacher, used to make him sit in the hall when he did it too much!" Jayson laughed. "We were all so jealous because we wanted to get out of her class so badly."

They continued with their conversation that way for another five minutes until Jayson tossed the green plastic bag at Moore.

"Here, my mom made me get you some crap," Jayson said.

"Thanks."

"Hey, did your dad really play for *that* team?"

"Yeah, he expects me to go there as well."

And Jayson realized the pressure Moore must be under to get that basketball scholarship.

And in only the way Jayson and Moore knew how to acknowledge the struggle that Moore was dealing with and for Jayson to show his support.

"Now one more round of Firepower Elite and I'm going to kick your ass, Moore."

CHAPTER 29

March was warmer than expected and most of the snow was starting to melt in the first week. The newspaper wanted to do an article on Sadie after she won the photo contest and she used the opportunity to try and raise more money for the shelter. Once the journalist realized she only entered the contest to raise the five thousand dollars to help fund extra beds in the shelter, she wanted to help Sadie spread awareness.

Her essay titled *The Whole Picture* wrote of the forgotten citizens in our city and how vulnerable they were. The mere act of living was survival for them, especially when the winter months came with their excruciatingly cold temperatures.

Sadie insisted on having the names of the four friends who helped her that day mentioned in the article. And along with their names, a photo of the five of them standing in front of St. Agatha's was printed on the front page of the paper.

The Main Street Shelter was able to raise more money than expected and not only had enough money for additional beds, but they were able to add an addition to an already too small facility.

The addition came with one added feature. The facility now had a main lounge area where those who wanted to get out of the cold, rain or sun, could come and take shelter in a safe place. It was agreed that the lounge would be named after the one person who was the inspiration for Sadie and her friends. Pesky Pete's Place was etched in a brass plaque and affixed to the door.

The school March break was one week away, and Mr. Crane informed the group that they no longer were committed to serving their detention at St. Agatha's.

"I think we can all agree that you four have proven your commitment and served your time," Mr. Crane said.

Jayson, Sadie, Lucy and Moore all agreed they wanted to stay on and continue to serve the visitors to the St. Agatha's Soup Kitchen. With one difference. Jonnie now wanted to join them on their days there.

Mr. Crane's eyes filled with tears and he began to say something to them, instead, he smiled at them and turned and walked to the kitchen and began to prepare some soup. Unable to speak.

CHAPTER 30

June came faster than Jayson thought it would and he surprised himself by being disappointed by the prospect of the end of school. When the year began, he thought the one hundred and ninety-six days would drag on like a prison sentence and his induction into a year-long detention made him want to quit school. Instead, he came face to face with three kids that he had nothing in common with and now considered to be his closest friends.

Lucy was leaving for the elite music camp in Toronto on July 7th and Sadie had shelved her black clothing for the summer and was committing herself to explore her photographic talent and had seemed to be over her crush on Moore.

Sadie promised to teach Jayson how to properly shoot a basketball and Jayson agreed to teach Sadie how to ride a skateboard. Sadie had gone from the frightening Goth Girl at the beginning of the year to his friend and confidante. Jonnie seemed to have permanently resolved to not embarrass himself in front of girls and proved, in the process, that he also had a great sense of humor. It was what his dad called a dry sense of humor, and he was freaking funny.

Moore finally admitted to the group that he was gay, but that he wasn't ready to tell his dad, or teammates, yet. He needed time to get the strength within himself to face his father and stand up to the image of what his father thought he should be. Until then, he counted on and needed their support.

Father Monahan assured Jayson that his doubts about himself or his place with religion were alright and that in any case he wouldn't be fated into damnation for asking questions.

The shelter had a ribbon cutting for the new addition to the facility that was now able to house fifty more beds thanks to Sadie donating her photo contest winnings, and Mr. Crane presented the four reprobates who ended up in detention in September with the citizenship award for 'exemplary service to their city'.

The mayor attended the school assembly to award the medals, with all their parents and friends watching on.

So, grade nine didn't suck after all and Jayson managed to survive the one hundred and ninety-six days at SOS.

Jayson emptied the contents of his locker into his backpack, tossing out his essays and scrap paper that accumulated at the bottom throughout the year.

His head was inside his locker when he heard the echo of the familiar taunt that followed him since that fated grade six gym class.

"Marshmallow," it was low, almost subtle, and if it hadn't grated on Jayson for so many years, even he would have missed it.

He stood up straight and looked around the hall. Most of the students had left for the day and Jayson locked eyes with one of the few people in the hall and the only one looking directly at him.

"You!" Jayson screamed. "Why can't you let it drop?"

Jayson was staring into the face of Stephanie Craymer. The one girl in Jayson's grade school who went further from not liking him, she scared him. Years of pushing him in line and correcting his mistakes in class mounted to this.

"What is with you?" Jayson asked. Not made nor angry, just frustrated.

Stephanie began to speak, and Jayson noticed her lower lip begin to quiver, "It's just a joke you know?"

"A joke? Ever since that day in gym class I have been called that horrible name behind my back," Jayson said. "Do you think that's funny?"

Stephanie stared at Jayson, unable to speak, "Well, no, I guess not. I was just being funny that day, I didn't realize it hurt you so much."

"You were the one who started that nickname?"

Stephanie nodded.

"Just stop it okay. We're in high school now," Jayson said, sounding dangerously close to being mature.

"Sure. Whatever," Stephanie turned to leave and then stopped and looked at Jayson. "Sorry, Jayson."

Jayson smiled and waved, and he watched the creator of his three-year torment walk away.

He slammed the locker shut, slipped his arms through his pack straps and flipped up his board with his feet, grabbing the wheels. He walked through the crowd of students and as he passed Moore he reached out and slapped his hand.

"Have a great summer, Moore."

"You too, buddy."

Jayson walked out the front door and dropped his board on the ground and wove his way down the path, around the other students of SOS who were leaving the school for the summer and stopped at the crosswalk.

His eyes locked with Jonah. The evil crossing guard, and Sadie's brother.

Jayson tapped the back of his board with his foot, popping the front up and grabbed hold of the wheels. He waited while Jonah stopped traffic and waved him across.

As he passed Jonah, Jayson nodded, "Until next year."

And Jonah pointed his two fingers at his eyes and then back towards Jayson, "I'll be here."

All in all, grade nine wasn't a total bust. Sure, James left, but he was coming in July for two weeks' vacation and had planned on spending the whole time at Jayson's house. Their friendship, as it turned out, wasn't lost. Shane had proven to be less of a pest than Jayson thought he was going to be at the beginning of the year, and Jayson was going to reward him by bringing him to the fort after school today. And two days earlier Jayson walked in on his mom tossing cans and packages that were the mainstay of her experimental cooking year into large green garbage bags, with his dad sitting close by grinning ear to ear.

His dad looked up at him and mouthed the words, 'steak tonight' and Jayson breathed a sigh of relief. His mom's revelation, as it turned out, followed Jayson's confession of what his grandmother burdened him with moments before she died. His mom realized the enormous pressure he had been under for the last year and vowed to be the one to tell his Aunt Alice what was said, and she promised it would never be brought up again. And they spent the whole night talking about what happened to Riley. Openly and honestly.

Finally, the burden of knowing that Aunt Alice and his mom had different fathers was released from his shoulders forever, and he could continue with his life. Relieved of Aunt Alice's attacks during family dinners.

Jayson stopped outside of Shane's school and waited for him to come out. Jayson knew he would be saying goodbye to his throngs of fans, so he would probably be one of the last ones to leave.

Jayson pulled out his phone and scrolled through the numerous posts that kids were announcing with the hashtag #lastday. Sadie, for the first time ever on her profile, posted a photo that included people. But not just any people. Four others were tagged. Lucy, Jonnie, Moore and Jayson. They were piled together, shoved into a selfie frame, caught off guard and in mid-laugh. Jayson liked it, reposted it, and then after scrolling through his feed he returned to the top of his profile.

Followers: 47 New Likes: 7

Jayson pocketed his phone and leaned against the tree. He learned over the year that although the pressure to be popular and to accumulate followers and likes was still strong, the true measure of his happiness was going to be the types of followers and the true likes he gained.

Moore had almost two thousand followers and he could only admit to having four close friends.

Jayson wasn't going to pretend to not still feel the pressure, he was, however, comfortable with where he was. But he was able to relax with the realization that just when you think you get it right, it all changes. And maybe that's not so bad.

Shane came running out of the school, and eager to get to the elusive fort that Jayson refused to previously show him, he jumped on his bike and rode towards where Jayson was waiting.

Together they weaved their way through students, parents and cars, careful not to hit any of them on their way.

They were on a mission.

While Jayson grew closer to his family, his new friends and his perception of the people he met at St. Agatha's he grew closer to himself.

And he was finally able to admit what made him happy.

The end.

Author's Note

Thank you for reading, and I sincerely hope you enjoyed '***UNfollowED***'. It was a complete joy to write this coming-of-age story about regular teens dealing with regular challenges in the honest heartfelt way that teenagers approach life.

They are the glimmer of hope in our world and they can teach us the way to lead – and to follow.

Don't ever think you are based on what others say you are. Be you. Be true. Be someone you would want to follow. And remember, you don't have to be one thing.

* * *

As an independently published author, I rely on you, the reader, to spread the word. So, if you enjoyed the book, please tell your friends and family, and if it isn't too much trouble, I would appreciate a brief review.

Thanks again.

My best to you and yours.

L.L. Abbott

A FURTHER NOTE FROM THE AUTHOR

According to Stats Canada an average of 4,000 people dies of suicide every year and it's the second leading cause of death in our country's youth. Suicide prevention is everyone's responsibility and it can be achieved with government supported programs, open discussions in schools and amongst family and friends. **UnfollowED** is a work of fiction, but the reality is many people are touched directly or indirectly by suicide. Anyone anywhere in any city, town or country can feel as if they may have nobody to reach out to. No one should ever feel they are alone or must suffer in silence. Let's keep talking about mental health issues and continue to reach out to those who we think may be suffering. If you or anyone you care about need help the following agencies can help, and you can always search for support in your area online.

- **Call 911**
- **Kids Help Phone**: 1-800-668-6868
    - Text CONNECT to 686868
- **Trans Lifeline**: 1-877-330-6366
- **Hope for Wellness Help Line**: 1-855-242-3310
- **Canada Suicide Prevention Service**: 1-833-456-4566 [available 24/7]
- **National Suicide Prevention Lifeline**
  ACROSS THE US 1-800-273-8255

Books by L.L. Abbott

Mystery & Suspense

Thrillers

Teen & Young Adult

General Fiction

Made in the USA
Monee, IL
13 August 2021

75624934R00132